Understanding and Producing Speech

Edward H. Matthei has taught linguistics and psychology at the University of California, Irvine, since 1979, when he gained his PhD in linguistics from the University of Massachusetts. His research interests are language development, psycholinguistics and neurolinguistics.

Thomas Roeper is professor of linguistics at the University of Massachusetts. After postgraduate studies at Harvard, he taught at the University of Chicago and for a year was a fellow of the MIT Sloan Center for Cognitive Studies. His special interests are language acquisition, psycholinguistics and morphology on which he has lectured in Japan, Canada and Europe and has written many articles.

Universe Introductions to Linguistics

Published

Language Change: Progress or Decay?   Jean Aitchison
Understanding and Producing Speech
  Edward Matthei and Thomas Roeper

Forthcoming

Language, Meaning and Context   John Lyons
Syntax Today   Keith Brown
Language and Society   William Downes

Edward Matthei and Thomas Roeper

Understanding and Producing Speech

UNIVERSE BOOKS
New York

Published in the United States of America in 1985
by Universe Books
381 Park Avenue South, New York, NY 10016

85 86 87 88 89 / 10 9 8 7 6 5 4 3 2 1

Printed in the United States of America

Library of Congress Cataloging in Publication Data

Matthei, Edward.
    Understanding and producing speech.

    Reprint. Originally published: London : Fontana
Paperbacks, 1983.
    Bibliography: p.
    Includes index.
    1. Speech. 2. Psycholinguistics. I. Roeper, Thomas.
II. Title. III. Series.
P95.M38   1985   401'.9   84-24123
ISBN 0-87663-457-9
ISBN 0-87663-873-6 (pbk.)

'The aspects of things that are most important for us are hidden because of their simplicity and familiarity (one is unable to notice something – because it is always before one's eyes).'

Ludwig Wittgenstein,
Philosophical Investigations

Contents

Introduction to Universe Linguistics   9

Preface   11

1   Introduction   13
2   The Vocal and Hearing Organs   21
3   Perceiving and Producing Speech Sounds   39
4   The Connection between Grammar and
    Speech   61
5   Assigning Grammatical Structures to
    Sentences   76
6   The Organization of Phrases   116
7   Producing Sentences   162
8   The Mental Lexicon   176
9   Conclusion   192

References   197
Index   205

Introduction to Universe Linguistics

In the past twenty-five years, linguistics—the systematic study of language—has come of age. It is a fast expanding and increasingly popular subject, which is now offered as a degree course at a number of universities. As a result of this expansion, psychologists, sociologists, philosophers, anthropologists, teachers, speech therapists and numerous others have realized that language is of crucial importance in their life and work. But when they tried to find out more about the subject, a major problem faced them—the technical and often narrow nature of much writing about linguistics.

The Universe Introductions to Linguistics series is an attempt to solve this problem by presenting current findings in a lucid and non-technical way. Its object is twofold. First, it hopes to outline the 'state of play' in certain crucial areas of the subject, concentrating on what is happening now, rather than on surveying the past. Secondly, it aims to show how linguistics links up with other disciplines such as sociology, psychology, philosophy, speech therapy and language teaching.

The series will, we hope, give readers a fuller understanding of the relationship between language and other aspects of human behavior, as well as equipping those who wish to find out more about the subject with a basis from which to read some of the more technical literature in textbooks and journals.

Jean Aitchison
London School of Economics

Preface

This book is written for anyone who is interested in language and in how we speak and comprehend. We have tried to provide an introduction to the psychological study of language that is clear and up-to-date. We have also tried to present our discussion in a coherent way, organizing the whole range of subjects around a few major themes. That is, we have tried to put things together so that something like a general theory of language use emerges as we go along. We feel that we have learned quite a bit through writing this book, and it is our hope that we have said some things that will be of interest to those who are familiar with the field as well as to those who have little or no experience in it.

Because the two of us have been on opposite sides of America for most of the time we spent in writing this book, we found it necessary to set up a division of labour. We wrote Chapter 1 together. Roeper took the responsibility for writing Chapters 4, 5 and 6. Matthei wrote Chapters 2, 3, 7, 8 and 9, and also took responsibility for overseeing the preparation of the final manuscript, making some minor stylistic revisions on Roeper's chapters to ensure that the book would 'speak with one voice'. We have enjoyed working with one another and would like to take this opportunity to thank each other. The collaboration has been an enjoyable one, and we have learned a lot from each other.

There are also others who deserve our thanks, among them the people whose experimentation we have discussed. However, we should point out that as we worked

Preface

through the experiments of others we found ourselves developing a few ideas of our own. For instance, the theory of unconstrained inferences and the separation of movement from control in parsing are ours (and so no blame should be heaped on others for these ideas).

Thanks also go to Chuck Clifton and Lyn Frazier of the University of Massachusetts who read and commented on a number of the chapters as they were being written. Robert Remez of Barnard College supplied us with the spectrogram which appears as Figure 4 in the text, and we wish to thank him for that as well as for many informal chats about speech perception and acoustic phonetics. We would also like to thank the Department of Linguistics at the University of Massachusetts, Amherst, and the School of Social Sciences at the University of California, Irvine, for providing an atmosphere in which our study of psycholinguistics could flourish. Thanks go to our colleagues at both places and to our students, many of whom encountered various sections of this book in their classes.

We also owe special thanks to Jean Aitchison, the series editor, for her comments on our chapter drafts and for her support for our efforts throughout the writing of this book. We didn't always follow her advice to the letter, but we learned quite a bit from our collaboration with her. One couldn't ask for a better editor.

Finally, we would like to thank the staff of the Word-processing Center at the School of Social Sciences at the University of California, Irvine, for the excellent job they did in preparing the manuscript, Cheryl Larson and Kathy Alberti in particular.

EM/TR

12

1. *Introduction*

Speaking and understanding the speech of others are things we do every day. Under normal circumstances we do these things effortlessly and, it seems, almost instantaneously. It takes almost no effort and very little, if any, conscious thought to turn our thoughts into words and sentences in order to communicate them to others; and, likewise, we ordinarily have no trouble in getting at the thoughts that others express in their words and sentences. It may seem surprising to some people, therefore, that the processes that underlie these remarkable abilities appear to be quite complex.

Every normal human uses language, and it is just this fact that makes it so easy for us to fall into the trap of thinking that there is little or nothing to be explained about our ability to use language. As we shall see, the systems that underlie our ability to use language must be quite complicated; and it is part of the goal of this book to show why this must be so, to show that any facile and transparent explanations of our linguistic abilities must necessarily be suspect.

Speaking and Understanding

Let us take a closer look at what goes on in producing and understanding a sentence. In taking this closer look, we will try to suggest where some of the complexity we have talked about must lie, and we will also take this as an opportunity to introduce some of the terminology we will need to use in later chapters. Suppose, for example, we wish to inform someone of a certain fact or state of affairs, say, that the absence of lettuce in our garden is due to the industriöus activity of a rabbit with a healthy appetite for cultivated salad greens. We might say, *A rabbit ate all of the lettuce*. Now, what must take place to enable us to utter this sentence?

To start off, we must find the words that we need in order to refer to the relevant aspects of the situation we wish to describe: *rabbit, ate, letuce*, etc. We will assume that this involves searching through some sort of list of the vocabulary items we know in order to pick out the words we need. This list we shall call our **mental lexicon**. The mental lexicon, we can imagine, will contain information much like that contained in a dictionary: information about the part of speech, the meaning and pronunciation of individual words, as well as information about any idiosyncrasies certain words might have, such as deviations from the normal rules for plural formation (e.g., *goose/ geese*) or restrictions on what kinds of sentences a particular word can appear in. The mental lexicon, then, will contain quite a bit of information about how and where a word is used. We will have more to say about the character of this information, and how it is organized, in later chapters.

Not only do we have to find the words we need, we also have to put them together into a sentence which will accurately describe the state of affairs to our listener. Just any old combination of words will not do. For example, the string of words, *rabbit all the a ate of lettuce*, is not a sentence; and it will not do the job, even though our listener, having observed the absence of lettuce in the garden, might be able to figure out our message by unscrambling our utterance as if it were some sort of anagram. The words that we have chosen must be put in a specific order if what we are to say is to be an English

14

sentence. The words must be put together so that they conform to the rules that govern the word and phrase patterns of English sentences. The set of rules which determines the order in which words are put together to form sentences is called the **syntax** of the language (see Chapters 4, 5 and 6). Thus, we might say, *A rabbit ate all of the lettuce*, or, *All of the lettuce was eaten by a rabbit*.

Other combinations of these words will be possible within the constraints imposed by the rules of English syntax, but not all of these will communicate the same message – the sentence, *All of the lettuce ate the rabbit*, for example. We must, then, not only choose a string of words that obeys the syntactic rules of English, i.e., a string of words that is a sentence; but we must also choose a sentence that means what we want it to mean. We can do this by referring to a set of **semantic rules**. This set of rules and principles will determine the meanings of sentences; that is, these rules describe how the different words in their different positions in the syntactic structure of a sentence play a role in determining the meaning of the sentence as a whole. This set of rules is not well understood at the present time, but we will have some things to say about them in the chapters which follow.

Now that we have chosen an appropriate sentence, we must say it. This process, too, involves some very complex planning. On the basis of how each of the words in our sentence is supposed to be pronounced – the **phonetic description** – we must send out a sequence of instructions to the hundreds of muscles which control our vocal apparatus. These instructions must be carefully planned and sequenced – a nontrivial problem, as we shall see in Chapter 3 – so that each of the sounds in the words in our sentence is articulated correctly and at the right time. The movements of our vocal apparatus cause small pressure changes in the air surrounding us. These pressure changes are **sound waves**. The whole process of converting a thought – the message – into a sequence of sounds is

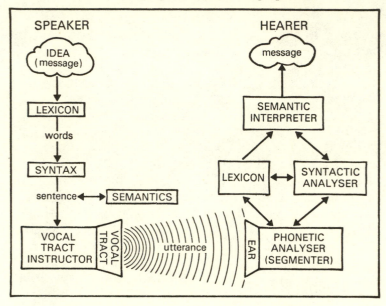

Fig. 1: A simplified model of the communication process

summarized in the 'Speaker' portion of Figure 1, above.

The sound waves we have produced travel through the air to our listener's ears. The pressure changes in the air activate our listener's hearing apparatus, and he or she will hear our message. Our listener will receive our message as a continuous stream of speech sounds something like this: *arabbitateallofthelettuce*. The first thing that our listener must do, therefore, is to divide this sequence of sounds into a sequence of words, checking this division against his or her mental lexicon to make sure that the division has been made in such a way that each packet of sounds corresponds to an actual English word. At this time our listener will also have an opportunity to determine the meanings of these words, as described in his or her mental lexicon. Then, or,

16

perhaps, at the same time, our listener must also figure out the syntactic structure of the sentence into which the words have been placed by the speaker, checking all the while to make sure that the structure he or she has been constructing conforms to the rules of English syntax. Armed with this combination of lexical and syntactic information gleaned from the utterance, our listener can then use the semantic rules to figure out the meaning of our utterance.

We have, of course, left out many things in our sketch of the processes of producing and comprehending a sentence. We have, for example, left out any consideration of how the situation in which our sentence was uttered may have helped our listener. If our listener had been with us in the garden and had noticed the absence of our carefully tended lettuce, he or she might have been able to deduce the content of our message once the word *rabbit* had come out of our mouths; and, thus, our listener might have been able to 'short-circuit' much of the comprehension process we have described. The **context** in which a sentence is uttered plays an undeniable role in determining the ease or 'depth' of processing involved in understanding a sentence. Unfortunately, very little is known about the way in which such essentially nonlinguistic information is used in understanding sentences. We have chosen, therefore, to discuss the effects of such information on the speech understanding process only in places in later chapters where it cannot be ignored.

We have chosen to do much the same with discussions of the ways in which sentences are strung together and integrated to form discourses and conversations. This, too, is an area in which researchers are just beginning to make headway, and little is known at this point. We will focus almost exclusively on the processes involved in producing and comprehending individual sentences in this book. But, just as words are the building blocks for sentences, sentences are the building blocks for discourses; and we would expect that what we say here about sentences will be a necessary part of what will be said about the ways that sentences are combined to construct appropriate discourses.

About 'Rules'

Before going any further, we should make some remarks about what we mean when we talk about 'rules' in our discussions. We assume that every person who speaks and understands sentences in a language knows that language, and we assume that a person who knows a language has, in some way, internalized – or learned – a grammar for that language. We assume, then, that people carry around in their heads a system of rules and principles that enables them to use their language, a system which determines the sound-meaning correspondences in that language. The linguist or psycholinguist, in discussing 'the rules' for a particular language, is making an hypothesis about what this system is like. It is obvious that people using a language appear to be following some set of rules, and the linguist or psycholinguist's talk of rules should be looked upon as an attempt to make explicit those rules that are apparent in the linguistic behaviour of language-users. In effect, the 'rules' of linguists or psycholinguists can be considered to be their best guesses as to the nature of the rules that language-users must have somewhere in their heads. For this reason, the words 'rule' and 'grammar' will be used interchangeably here to refer both to the representation of language inside a person's head and to the linguist or psycholinguist's model or guess about the nature of that representation.

The reader should keep this distinction in mind in the chapters which follow, because it is an important one. But it is our hope that this ambiguity in use will not cause any confusion. When these words arise in the course of our

18

discussions it should be clear in which sense we intend them.

Overview of the Chapters to Come

Our discussion in the next chapters will proceed as follows. Chapters 2 and 3 deal with the sounds of speech. We will consider the way in which speech sounds are made by speakers, and we will also describe certain acoustic properties of those sounds as well as the processes that are involved in perceiving those sounds as speech. Chapters 4, 5 and 6 deal with syntactic structure. In these chapters we consider the evidence that syntactic structure is something that people use in understanding and producing speech, and we focus on the problems involved in assigning syntactic structures to strings of words – the parsing problem. These chapters will deal almost exclusively with the processes that occur in listening. Chapter 7 deals with sentence production, and in it we will have a look at how we plan sentences before saying them and at how our plans can sometimes go awry. Chapter 8 deals with the lexicon: the sorts of information it must contain and how that information might be organized so that it can be used efficiently in understanding and producing sentences. Chapter 9 is essentially a recapitulation of the earlier chapters, a summary of what we take to be the important issues we have raised in the preceding chapters.

One final note is in order before we jump right into the next chapter: this book is not intended to be a treatise on understanding and producing speech. We have not tried to cover everything, nor have we attempted to cover every-thing we do talk about with the same amount of depth and rigour. We have tried, as far as possible, to present a coherent view, an approach to a theory with a certain structure. As such, our presentation is somewhat biased by our beliefs about what kind of theory will be needed eventually to explain our ability to use language. However, we encourage our readers to go beyond the somewhat limited scope of this little book to explore in depth the issues raised here.

2. *The Vocal and Hearing Organs*

Speech Production: the Vocal Organs

The physiological structures that we use to produce speech sounds all have other functions. We use the tongue and lips in eating and swallowing, we use the lungs and windpipe in breathing, and so on. These physiological structures are also possessed by other animals. This has led many to say that speech is what is known as an 'overlaid function'. That is, human beings, as a species, have evolved to make use of old or pre-existing structures to serve a new function. There are important differences in both the structure and functioning of these physiological structures in human beings, however. The musculature connected to the tongue and lips in human beings, for example, is more highly developed and more agile than the corresponding structures in other animals. This increased flexibility and control is of no use whatsoever in eating and swallowing – in fact, certain characteristics of these structures in humans actually make for less efficient eating and swallowing. But this increased flexibility and control is extremely useful for producing rapid and articulate speech.

The raw material, so to speak, for speech production is the steady stream of air that comes out of our lungs as we exhale. Most of the time, of course, we make little or no noise as we exhale; but if we set the air coming out of our lungs into rapid vibration, the movement of this air becomes audible. This happens unintentionally when we snore, and it also happens intentionally when we speak.

The source of this rapid vibration of air in speech production is, most often, the vocal cords.

The **vocal cords** are contained in the **larynx**, which lies behind the chunk of cartilage you can feel in your neck (the 'Adam's apple'); and they form an adjustable 'gate' across the passageway coming out of our lungs. When they are open, air passes steadily from the lungs into the vocal tract; but they can be closed to shut off the flow of air from the lungs. When we are speaking, the vocal cords open and close rapidly, breaking the air stream into a quick series of short bursts. This series of bursts can be heard as a sort of buzzing sound which sounds 'higher' as the rate of vibration of the vocal cords is increased. (You can produce this kind of sound by putting your tongue between your lips and then forcing air between your tongue and lips; the sound you produce is what is commonly called 'the raspberry'.) The character of this buzzing sound that is produced by the vocal cords is affected by the shape of the vocal tract; the **vocal tract** is the intricately shaped passageway that lies above the larynx, and it is made up of the **pharynx**, the **mouth** and its parts, and the **nasal cavity**. A change in the shape of the vocal tract will cause a change in the character of the sound we hear. Those familiar with reeded musical instruments may have noticed that this way of making sounds is identical to the way that instruments like the clarinet or oboe work: the musician blows air on to the reed(s), which produces a kind of buzzing noise, and the body of the instrument with its various configurations of open and closed valves then modifies the character of the buzz to produce different notes.

The air stream coming out of the lungs, then, provides the energy needed for producing speech sounds. The vocal cords convert this energy into a buzzing sound that we can hear. And, finally, movements of the **tongue**, **lips** and **velum**, by changing the shape of the vocal tract, turn the buzz into different and distinguishable speech sounds.

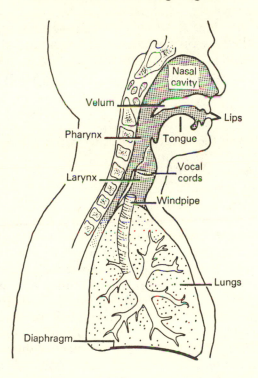

Fig. 2: Diagram showing the parts of the body involved in speech production

Most speech sounds are made in this way. There are, however, a few other methods we have for producing audible sounds from the lungs' air stream. One way is to make the vocal tract quite narrow at some point along its length – we usually do this by moving the tongue up in the mouth so that the vocal tract is almost blocked, or by almost closing the lips. Air that passes through this narrow space becomes turbulent like the air coming out of a puncture in a bicycle tyre; and this turbulence is heard as a hissing sound. This is how we produce sounds with a hissing quality like *s*, *sh* and *f*. Such sounds are called **fricatives**, they are produced by creating a kind of friction in the air stream. (Notice that this kind of sound is very much-like the sound we hear when we rub a surface with sandpaper.)

Another method for producing speech sounds is to cut off briefly the flow of air through the vocal tract altogether. We usually use the tongue or lips to make the block. Air pressure builds up behind the blocked place and then rushes out when the blockage is removed. This technique is used when we produce sounds like *p*, *t* or *k*. These sounds are aptly named **stop consonants**.

You should notice that we can make fricatives and stop consonants with or without vibrating our vocal cords. Speech sounds that we produce with our vocal cords vibrating are called **voiced**; those produced without simultaneous vocal cord vibration are called **unvoiced**. We can have, therefore, voiced and unvoiced forms of fricatives and stop consonants. In English we have voiced and unvoiced pairs like *z* vs *s* (*zap/sap*) and *b* vs *p* (*bump/ pump*). These sounds differ from each other only in whether they are produced with vocal cord vibration or not. (You can feel the vocal cord vibration by placing your finger on your larynx. When you say the pair *zap/sap* you should be able to feel vibration when you say the *z* and no vibration when you say the *s*.)

We will mention here three other methods that can be used in speech production. We can **whisper**, which is like producing a hissing sound. In whispering, we produce the hiss by holding the vocal cords close together and not vibrating them. (Thus, all whispered speech is unvoiced.) We can also produce '**clicks**' by blocking the vocal tract in two places at once, sucking the air out from between the two blocks, and then quickly releasing both blocks. Sounds like these are used in some African languages, but they are not used in English words. The sound used to indicate mild

24

disapproval that is most often spelled 'tsk' in English is a 'click'. For completeness, we also mention that some languages use sounds that are produced while inhaling; such speech sounds are called **implosives**. However, English speech sounds are normally produced only while exhaling.

The Articulation of Some English Speech Sounds

Changing the shape of the vocal tract to produce speech sounds is called **articulation**. It is customary to describe the various speech sounds in terms of the movements of the tongue, lips etc. that are used to produce them; that is, speech sounds are described in terms of the articulatory movements associated with their production.

Speech sounds are usually divided up into two classes: the **vowels** and the **consonants**. We can characterize the difference between these two classes of sounds by looking at the different kinds of articulatory movements that are used to produce the sounds in each class. When we produce vowels, we leave the vocal tract relatively free of obstructions; thus, the air flows freely out of the lungs and mouth. We make consonants by interrupting or impeding the flow of air through the vocal tract. Consonants are articulated by placing obstructions in the vocal tract with the tongue or lips. To simplify things a bit, we might say that vowels are the steady-state sounds in the speech stream and that consonants are interruptions in the stream.

We describe the articulation of vowels in terms of tongue and lip position. We make different vowel sounds by moving the tongue up and down and back and forth in the mouth and by spreading or rounding the lips. Say the pair *boo/bee* to yourself. You will notice two things. When you articulate the *oo* sound in *boo* your lips are pushed out somewhat and rounded, but in articulating the *ee* sound in *bee* your lips are pulled back somewhat and spread. You will also notice that in pronouncing the *oo* your tongue is raised quite high in the back of your mouth. In pronouncing the *ee* your tongue remains high in your mouth and moves forward almost to your teeth. (We should note here that the tongue is extremely mobile: you can move the tip, the edges and the main body of the tongue independently. When we describe the **tongue position** for vowel articulation, we will be referring to the place where the main part – or **body** – of the tongue is in the mouth. Thus, in the descriptions of the vowels which follow, we will take tongue position to be the place where the body of the tongue is highest in the mouth.)

We can systematically identify the vowels, then, by describing the relative position that the tongue takes while they are being made. The *ee* sound in *bee* is a high front vowel, and we would write the word phonetically as [bi].[1] The *oo* is a high back vowel, and we would write *boo* phonetically as [bu].

Certain vowel sounds of English are made up of combinations of vowel sounds. Such vowel sounds are called **diphthongs** or **vocalic glides**. Three common glides found in English are [aɪ], as in *ride*, [raɪd], [aʊ], as in *cow*, [kaʊ], and [ɔɪ], as in *boy*, [bɔɪ]. If you listen carefully, you will probably be able to discover other glides in your own speech and the speech of others.

In principle, any lip position can be used with any tongue position. In English, however, only the back vowels are made with rounded lips. Native speakers of English often find it difficult to go against this 'rule' when they are learning a foreign language. For example, French has a high front rounded vowel – the vowel in the French word for 'street', *rue*; and many English speakers find this vowel sound particularly elusive when they attempt to learn the

---

1. We follow here the custom of putting phonetic representations inside square brackets. For the phonetic transcription, we have used the symbols of the IPA (International Phonetic Alphabet).

language. Russian has a high back *un*rounded vowel which many English speakers also find difficult to master. Articulatory habits, once they have become established, seem to be quite difficult to overcome.

Finally, most speakers of English raise the velum during vowel production, thus shutting off the flow of air through the nasal cavity; others may leave it partially lowered. The added nasal quality that leaving the velum lowered contributes to vowel sounds is not used to distinguish one English vowel sound from another, but it is used for this purpose in other languages, as in the French *bon/beau*.

A final note is in order here. The vocal tract configurations that we find described in textbooks are idealized, and a fair amount of deviation from these idealized positions occurs when we are stringing sounds together in connected speech. There is a certain amount of variability in the way these sounds are articulated by individual speakers as well. Most of the deviations from these ideal positions occur because of the influence of other sounds that come before or after the sound being made. The tongue cannot move from one position to another instantaneously, so often it doesn't quite get to the ideal position before we start moving it to the position for the next sound. For example, the *k* sound is made by pressing the back of the tongue up against the back of the roof of the mouth. Just where the tongue is placed, however, depends to a certain extent on what the following vowel is. If you say the words *cool/key* you will notice – by saying the words slowly and noting carefully the position of your tongue – that your tongue is slightly more forward in your mouth when you articulate the *k* sound in *key* than it is when you articulate the *k* sound in *cool*. In this example, it is the position of the vowel that follows the sound which influences the point of articulation. A similar kind of influence can be observed in the pair *slip/sloop*. You will notice in saying this pair that you start rounding your lips for the *oo* sound in *sloop* during the articulation of the *sl* cluster at the beginning of that word. This rounding 'colours' the sound of the *sl* cluster somewhat, but it does not cause us any difficulties in hearing the cluster as *sl*. Finally, in fast speech we often just start the articulatory gesture for a sound, i.e., we move our tongue and lips *toward* the ideal position, and then go on to articulate the next sound without finishing the articulatory movements. Despite all of these variations from the ideal positions, we have little or no trouble in understanding speech.

With this brief description of the speech production apparatus and the ways in which different vocal tract configurations are associated with different speech sounds behind us, we will now go on to discuss the way in which the ear receives and analyses speech sounds. After this we will go on to describe how the different vocal tract positions we discussed in this section are related to the acoustic characteristics of the speech sounds we hear.

Speech Reception: the Hearing Sense Organs

The physical function of the ear is to receive acoustic vibrations (sounds) and to convert them into signals that are suitable for transmission along the auditory nerve to the appropriate part of the brain for analysis. The complex processing of these signals that occurs in the brain 'creates' the perceptual world of sound. In this section, we will describe the anatomy and physiology of the ear from its external parts to the point where sound stimuli are converted into nerve impulses to be sent to the brain. This aspect of the hearing process we will call **sound reception**. The analysis of the sounds we hear that occurs further along in the hearing process we will call **sound perception**; this will be the subject of a later section. The processes which take place in the ear are quite complex. However, we will try to simplify things as much as possible. Our purpose here is simply to provide a very general description of what goes on in the ear when we hear sounds and to characterize the kind of information that the ear extracts from the world of sound. (Those interested in a more detailed description of the ear should consult Denes and Pinson, 1973, Chapter 5.)

The ear. In considering what happens in the ear, we will find it useful to divide the ear up into three parts: the outer ear, the middle ear and the inner ear. Figure 3 gives a somewhat simplified picture of the ear upon which these areas are marked.

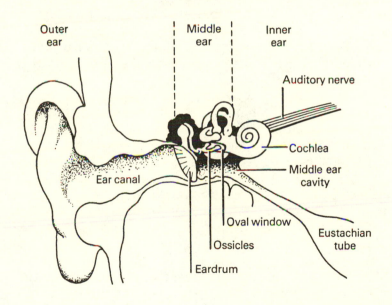

Fig. 3: Simplified cut-away view of the ear

29

The outer ear. The **outer ear** consists of the outside (visible) portions of the ear and the **ear canal**. It plays a relatively minor role in the hearing process. The ear canal is a passageway about 2.5 cm long (1 inch) which is closed at one end by the **eardrum** and open to the outside world at the other end. Sound waves which fall on the external parts of the ear are funnelled down the ear canal where they set the eardrum into vibration. The ear canal acts as an acoustic resonator and serves to amplify the sounds a bit, thus causing the eardrum to vibrate somewhat more than it would if it were located right on the side of our heads. This enables us to hear sounds that we might not hear if we had our eardrums on the outside of our skulls. The position of the eardrum also helps to protect this delicate structure from injury and keeps the temperature and humidity around it relatively free from the kinds of variation it would be exposed to if it were located on the outside of the skull.

The middle ear. The **middle ear** contains three small bones, called the **auditory ossicles**, that form a mechanical link between the eardrum and the inner ear. These bones are suspended in a cavity in the skull, and they transmit motions of the eardrum to a membrane called the **oval window**, which stretches across the entrance to the inner ear. The middle ear's main function is to increase the amount of vibrational energy that is transmitted to the inner ear. If we were to remove the eardrum and ossicles so that sound waves impinged directly on the oval window, almost all of the sound energy that came into the ear would be reflected off the oval window, just as sound bounces off any relatively hard surface. The ossicles are set up so that they amplify the vibrations of the eardrum as they transmit them to the oval window. It is estimated that this set-up makes the vibrations reaching the oval window about 35 times stronger than they would be if the eardrum and ossicles were not present (Denes and Pinson, 1973, p. 89).

The middle ear also contains mechanisms to protect the inner ear from extremely loud sounds. Unfortunately, these mechanisms do not work instantaneously, and sudden, very loud sounds can do permanent damage to our hearing.

The inner ear. It is in the **inner ear** that the vibrations produced by sound waves are finally converted into nerve impulses. The structure which looks like a snail's shell in Figure 3, called the **cochlea**, is responsible for this. The cochlea is a membrane structure filled with fluid. When the ossicles push on the oval window, the fluid in this chamber is pushed about and put into vibration. A series of **hair cells** located in the membrane of the cochlea are caused to bend by this vibration. The hair cells are located close to the endings of nerve fibres from the **auditory nerve**. When the hair cells are bent, they stimulate these fibres, which then transmit this information to the brain along the auditory nerve. The way in which the hair cells stimulate the nerve fibres is not completely understood at this time.

It has been shown that the information which is transmitted to the brain is essentially a frequency vs intensity vs time analysis of incoming sound waves. The ear, then, transmits information about how loud the sounds at certain pitches are and how this varies over time. (Cf. von Békésy, 1960.)

The Acoustics of Speech Sounds

In the preceding sections we discussed the ways in which we make various speech sounds and the way in which the ear picks up and analyses sound. We turn now to a description of the sounds themselves. Speech sounds are not like pure tones or simple musical notes. The sounds produced by the vocal tract are made up of sounds at a number of different frequencies – or pitches – and of different intensities, all produced simultaneously; and the flow of speech is continuous, so that the individual sounds in the speech stream blend together and affect each other in subtle ways, as we noted above. This produces some problems in the analysis of speech sounds and also, as we shall see later, poses some interesting problems for us when we set out to explain how it is that people are able to perceive speech in the rapid and apparently effortless way that they do.

The vocal tract as an acoustic filter. We noted earlier that different vocal tract configurations change the character of the buzzing sound that is produced by the vocal cords. This is because the vocal tract acts as a **resonating chamber** which selectively reinforces and intensifies certain frequencies in the buzzing sound. The frequencies that are reinforced are determined by the length and shape of this resonating chamber (by the cross-sectional area as a function of distance from the glottis, to be exact), and, thus, changes in the shape of the vocal tract will cause changes in the frequencies that are reinforced. The frequencies that are reinforced are known as the **resonant frequencies**.

We have all had experience with this kind of acoustic filter. In fact, we often use information we get from such filters in daily life. The best example of this can be found in the filling of a bottle with water from the tap. If we let the water from the tap splash into the sink we hear what is called 'white noise'; that is, the splashing water produces sound at all sorts of frequencies. Now, if we let the water run into a bottle the sound changes. This is because the bottle acts as a resonating chamber, and it selectively reinforces certain frequencies in the sound made by the water splashing in the bottle. As the bottle fills with water we hear the sound change in pitch. This happens because

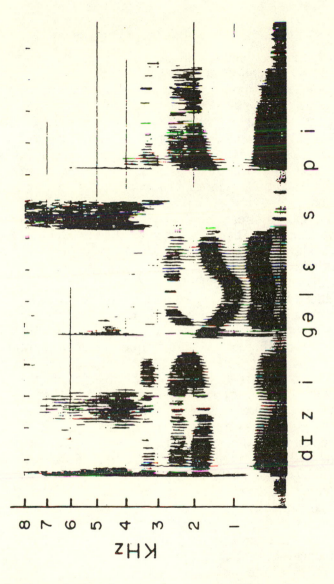

Fig. 4: A reproduction of an actual spectrogram. The graph represents the spectral analysis of an American male saying 'Dizzy Gillespie'. The vertical axis is a logarithmic scale, marked off in steps of one kilohertz (kHz); 1 kHz = 1000 Hz. (Courtesy of R. E. Remez)

the resonating chamber is changing in shape. As the air space gets smaller at the top of the bottle higher frequencies are reinforced, and we can hear the bottle filling up as the sound gets higher in pitch. With a little practice, we can tell when to turn off the tap without looking at the level of water in the bottle. The vocal tract works in essentially the same way as our bottle, although, of course, the vocal tract has a more complex shape than a bottle and therefore produces more complicated sounds.

The speech stream can be broken up into its various components in order to determine the specific elements that make up each speech sound. The most common way to do this is to make a **sound spectrogram**. A special machine has been developed to show how the sounds produced by the vocal tract vary from instant to instant. This machine, the **sound spectrograph**, transforms speech sounds into a graphic pattern on a piece of paper, a spectrogram. Figure 4 is an example of a spectrogram. It shows the changes in the frequency and intensity of the sounds in speech as time passes; thus, a spectrogram contains the same information that the ear transmits to the brain. The vertical axis of the spectrogram (see Figure 4) represents increasing sound wave frequencies; so the higher the pitch of a sound, the higher up on the paper it is marked. The intensity, or loudness, of the sound is shown by how dark the marking on the paper is at a given frequency. A dark band on the paper indicates that there is a fair amount of acoustic energy concentrated at the frequencies indicated on the vertical axis; a white area indicates that there is no sound being produced at the frequencies indicated on the vertical axis. The horizontal axis indicates the passage of time, and it is read from left to right.

The vowels. Vowels show up on a speech spectrogram as dark horizontal bands (see Figure 4) which correspond to steady-state concentrations of sound at certain frequencies. These bands of sound are called **formants**, and they correspond to the resonant frequencies of the vocal tract configurations used to produce them. It is common practice to number the formants from the bottom of the spectrogram to the top. The primary cues for speech recognition appear to lie in information carried in the first and second formants (F_1 and F_2). The telephone, for example, only gives us enough of a slice of the speech spectrum to identify reliably the first and second formants of many people's speech, and we normally have little trouble in understanding someone over the telephone.

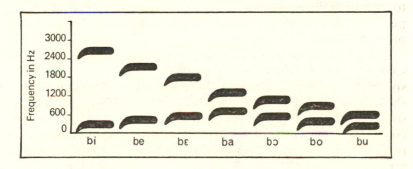

Fig. 5: Schematic diagram showing the relations between the first and second formants (F_1 and F_2) for seven English vowels (after Delattre, Liberman and Cooper, 1955)

In general, when we place the tongue high in the mouth during vowel articulation the frequency of the first formant (F_1) is lowered. Placing the tongue back in the mouth lowers the second formant (F_2). Thus, for the high front vowel [i], as in *bee*, the first two formants will be maximally separated. (A look at the simplified spectrograms in Figure 5 will help you to see this.) For the low central vowel [a], as in some pronunciations of the word *father*, the first two formants will be maximally centred. And, finally, for the

35

high back vowel [u], as in *boot*, the first two formants will be maximally lowered. The other vowels fall in between these values, as is illustrated in Figure 5. These three vowels, then, might be said to form the boundaries of the 'vowel space'; and it turns out that the three vowels [i], [a], [u] appear to play an important role in the speech perception process because of their roles as 'definers' of the vowel space.

To sum up, then, vowels are characterized as steady-state concentrations of sound energy at certain points in the sound spectrum. The vowels are distinguished from one another primarily by differences in the relation between their first and second formants, and these differences are determined by the differences in tongue position associated with their articulation. We turn now to the consonants.

The consonants. The effects of consonant articulation show up primarily in the ways that these vocal tract movements affect the vowels that follow them. To be more specific, they show up on a speech spectrogram as upward and downward swings at the beginnings of vowel formants; these swings are called **formant transitions**.

For stop consonants it appears that the length and direction of the formant transition into the second vowel formant (F_2) is a primary cue for the recognition of these sounds. (See Figures 4 and 5.) It is interesting to note that consonants do not appear in isolation from vowels; i.e., there is no time slice in the speech stream that can be heard as a stop consonant alone. If we take a piece of tape on which we have recorded the syllable [ba], for example, and start cutting off pieces of the tape from the consonant end, we eventually end up with a piece of tape on which just the vowel [a] is heard. But, if we cut the tape from the vowel end, we never get to a point where just the [b] sound is heard. As we cut pieces off, the syllable will get shorter and shorter until it suddenly turns into a sound like a chirp (the

36

formant transition), a sound that doesn't even sound like speech, let alone a [b]. This should not be surprising because you will notice that it is impossible to say a [b] without making it part of a syllable: you can say [ba], [bi], [bo], [bu] etc.; but you will never be able to say just [b]. The syllable, then, appears to be the minimal unit for speech production and speech perception.

Stop consonants in syllable-initial position also have an additional cue, which is the presence of a 'burst' at the onset of the syllable. This burst shows up on the spectrogram as a kind of blot in the upper frequency range. The burst corresponds to the puff of air that is produced when the stop is released. (See Figure 4.) The burst appears in different frequency ranges depending on which consonant is being articulated. This burst, together with the formant transition, appears to be a primary cue for stop consonant recognition. It has been shown, however, that either cue alone, under controlled conditions, is sufficient for discriminating one stop consonant from another. That is, there is a certain amount of redundancy in the speech signal.

The difference between voiced and unvoiced stop consonants shows up on a spectrogram as a difference between the onsets of the first and second formants. In a voiced consonant both F_1 and F_2 start at the same time. In unvoiced consonants the onset of the first formant (F_1) is delayed for about 40 or 50 msec. (.04 sec.). This difference corresponds to the delay in vocal cord vibration that occurs when we make unvoiced consonants. As far as we know, this is the only acoustic cue that distinguishes voiced from unvoiced consonants.

The hissing sound which characterizes the fricative consonants shows up as a band of relatively random acoustic energy in the higher frequencies in the spectrogram. It appears as a kind of fuzz in the upper portion of the graph. (See Figure 4.) The different fricative consonants are distinguished from one another by the range at which this fuzz appears. The noise appears between 1500 and 1700 Hz for the [f] sound, for example, and above 3500 Hz for the [s] sound.

In closing our discussion of the consonants, we will also mention that sometimes no sound at all can be a cue for consonant recognition. If, for example, we take a piece of tape on which we have recorded the word *slit* and splice in a small piece of blank tape between the [s] and [l] sounds, we will not hear the word *slit* with a slight pause between the [s] and [l] but instead the word *split*. That is, in certain positions in words we perceive a little stretch of silence as the consonant [p] (Liberman, Harris, Eimas, Lisker and Bastian, 1961). If we do the same thing with the word *sore*, splicing in a bit of silence between the [s] and [o], however, we get different results. In this case we hear not *spore* but *store*; so a slight pause in a different position will be perceived as a [t] (Bastian, Eimas and Liberman, 1961). These examples point out some of the many problems we encounter when we try to account for our ability to understand speech.

3. *Perceiving and Producing Speech Sounds*

When you stop to think about it, it doesn't seem that we should have a whole lot of trouble constructing a model of human speech perception. After all, we hear speech as a sequence of individual sound segments, strung together one after the other like beads on a string. It would appear, therefore, that the real work we would have to do in building our model would involve looking for the characteristic 'mark' that each sound segment makes in the speech stream. After we had this information it would be relatively easy – perhaps almost trivial – to design a set of filters, feature detectors or acoustic templates that would pick out the individual sound segments in the speech stream and identify them. A nice, relatively simple theory – very pleasing, in fact. Unfortunately, this simple theory appears to be quite wrong. Evidence from many experiments indicates that the acoustic patterns associated with speech sound segments are not strung together like beads on a string, each with its own little identifying mark, just waiting for the perceiver to read them off one by one.

There is a metaphor that gets trotted out quite a lot to explain what speech perception must be like. The identification of speech sounds is likened to the process of identifying the perpetrator of a crime. In the metaphor, the simple model we discussed above can be compared to solving a crime where the criminal has left his or her fingerprint. The detective can solve this sort of crime simply by comparing the fingerprint found at the scene of the crime to the fingerprints in a file of suspects. A match

of fingerprints identifies the criminal. However, as we mentioned, the experimental evidence indicates that speech perception cannot simply be a matter of matching acoustic fingerprints to sound segment criminals. It appears, instead, that when we perceive speech we are in a situation in which a specific clue might have been left by any one of a number of different criminals or in which a specific criminal might have left any number of different clues. (We discussed an example of the first sort of situation above when we saw that a bit of silence will be heard as either a [p] or a [t] when it occurs between two sounds in a word, depending on what the sounds are that occur before and after it.) The processes involved in speech perception seem to be more like those involved when the master detective deduces the identity of the criminal from a seemingly disparate array of data. The master detective *actively reconstructs* the sequence of events involved in the crime by looking at all the clues and noting the relations between them. The detective essentially adds information to the physical evidence by drawing upon his own experience. In perceiving speech we actively reconstruct the sequence of sound segments that must have been uttered by the speaker by taking the clues given in the sound waves we hear and adding to this information by drawing upon our knowledge of how our language works and, it appears, by also drawing upon what we know about how speech sounds are made. The information we get from the sound waves, then, is a kind of framework upon which we construct – or reconstruct – the message.

The Perceptual Unit: What Do We Hear?

The rate at which meaningful sound distinctions are transmitted in human speech is very rapid. Philip Lieberman (1973) points out that sound segments come at us at the rate of about 20 to 30 segments per second. That is, the phonetic distinctions that enable us to hear the word *bat* ([b], [æ], [t]) are transmitted, identified and stored at the rate of 20–30 segments a second. This is a puzzling fact, however. The fastest rate at which we can reliably identify individual sounds in sequence is only about 7 to 9 per second (Liberman, 1970). Sounds which come at us at the rate of 20 per second (or faster) merge into something like a tone in which each separate segment can no longer be distinguished. Our visual system has the same limitation, and that is why motion pictures work. A movie projector presents us with individual still images at a speed of 16 frames per second or greater; because this rate is higher than the rate at which we can perceive individual images, the images merge, and the perceived effect is that of smoothly flowing motion in the images on·the screen. If information about individual sound segments comes at us too quickly to enable us to identify the segments one by one, how, then, are we able to perceive speech?

The answer to this question appears to be that we don't perceive speech segment by segment. A number of studies done in the 1950s provided dramatic evidence for this. An enormous amount of time and money was spent in the 1950s on attempts to construct a reading maching for the blind (see Harris, 1953, or Peterson *et al.*, 1958, for example). One approach that was taken seemed to have promise: if phonetic segments are like beads on a string, then it ought to be possible to make a machine which would essentially 'glue' phonetic elements together to make words. A set of words, carefully pronounced by some speaker, was recorded on magnetic tape. Next, attempts were made to isolate the individual sound segments on the tape. The isolated sounds were then stored in a machine that would put them together to form new words. Systems of this sort turned out to be just about useless. The 'speech' which they produced was unintelligible, for all practical purposes; and in many cases the prerecorded segments seemed to take on different phonetic values when they

41

were put together to form new words; for example, what sounded like a [p] in the original recorded speech sometimes would sound like a [k] when it was put together with different sounds (cf. Cooper *et al.*, 1952).

That these attempts failed should not be surprising, since we noted earlier that it is impossible to isolate acoustically a piece of sound recording that is heard as a [b], for example, just as it is impossible for us to make a [b] without a vowel before or after it. We simply can't make or hear a [b] if it is not part of a syllable. The evidence is that the individual sounds in a word like [bæt], *bat*, are all squashed together into a single, syllable-sized unit. Consider what happens when we say 'bat'. We start with our vocal tract in the position characteristic of the [b], but we don't maintain this position. We immediately move our articulators toward the position they need to be in to make the vowel sound [æ], but we never quite get there because we start moving toward the [t] position before we reach the ideal 'steady-state' position for the vowel. The separate articulatory positions for each isolated segment are never quite reached; instead, all of the articulatory movements are rolled up into a composite articulatory movement that is characteristic of the syllable as a whole. This does not mean that the individual sound segments have no 'psychological status' for speech production, however: the sound segments can be looked upon as the units used in the instructions given to the vocal tract.

Just as we cannot separate the distinct articulatory gestures in the production of a syllable, we cannot separate the acoustic cues that are produced by each of the separate gestures. Thus, the sound pattern that results from the articulation of a syllable is a composite. The acoustic cues for the initial and final consonants appear, for the most part, because of the effects that their articulation have on the vowel (see the discussion of formant transitions, above). Lieberman (1975) has pointed out that this is, in effect, a system for time compression: 'the acoustic cues that characterize the initial and final consonants are transmitted in the time slot that would have been necessary to transmit a single isolated vowel' (p. 9). This appears to account for how we accomplish the high rate of information transmission in speech – we send out and receive information in syllable-sized units. According to one theory, we 'decode' the speech signal in terms of the articulatory movements that were put together to make the signal. Individual sounds, even though they have no independent acoustic status, are heard as discrete sounds. It appears, then, that speech perception requires us to make use of some sort of 'knowledge' that we have about the acoustic effects of articulatory movements as they interact in speech production (Liberman *et al.*, 1967; Lieberman, 1970).

Phonetic and 'Personal' Qualities of Speech Sounds

In the preceding section we noted that speech appears to be transmitted and decoded in syllable-sized units. The phonetic elements of each syllable are put together into a single acoustic pattern which is then 'unpacked' by the listener to yield the phonetic representation of the syllable. We also noted that, at least for consonants, a simple beads-on-a-string model of speech perception and production could not work. The reason for this is that the acoustic cues appropriate for the recognition of a given consonant in one syllable may be radically different from the acoustic cues appropriate for the recognition of the same consonant in a different syllable. Thus, there is a discouraging lack of **acoustic variance** in the speech signal.

There are other sources of invariance, too. In most early studies of speech production/recognition the problem of interspeaker variation was largely ignored. It turns out that when we take such variation into account we find that the acoustic pattern of a given speech sound uttered by one speaker may be quite different from the acoustic pattern that results when a different speaker says the same sound. This is especially dramatic when we observe the spectrographic patterns of speech sounds produced by children: the acoustic patterns for children and adults producing the same words are remarkably dissimilar (see the spectrograms reproduced in Lenneberg, 1967, for example). It appears, then, that we must somehow 'relativize' our criteria for speech sound identification to the general acoustic properties of a speaker's voice. That is, we must somehow be able to take into account what Ladefoged (1967) has referred to as the '**personal qualities**' of a speaker's voice in determining the phonetic content of his/her utterances.

Ladefoged and Broadbent (1957) provided dramatic experimental evidence of this. In their experiment, Ladefoged and Broadbent played a series of (synthesized) syllables to listeners. Listeners heard the sentence *Please say what this word is*, followed by one of the syllables. The fundamental frequency of the introductory sentence was varied so that the sentence appeared to be spoken by different speakers; the fundamental frequencies of the test syllables were not varied. Ladefoged and Broadbent found that the same syllable was heard to have different vowels, depending on which 'speaker' spoke the introductory sentence. For example, a syllable heard as *hit* when it followed the introductory sentence spoken by one 'speaker' was heard as *het* when it followed the sentence spoken by a different 'speaker'. Evidently, the listeners analysed the syllables in terms of their relations to the different properties of the introducing voices. According to Ladefoged and Broadbent, 'The linguistic information conveyed by a vowel sound does not depend on the absolute values of its formant frequencies, but on the relationship between the formant frequencies for that vowel and the formant frequencies of other vowels pronounced by that speaker' (p. 98).

44

Peterson and Barney (1952) recorded the speech of 76 speakers (33 men, 28 women and 15 children) as they read two lists of ten words. Peterson and Barney then measured and plotted the first two formant frequencies of the vowels their speakers produced. The results of their analyses are summarized in Figure 6. The data points (not shown in Figure 6) were labelled with the phonetic symbols of the vowels the speakers intended to convey. The loops in

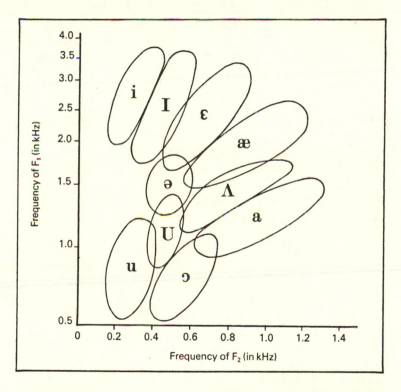

Fig. 6: Diagram showing the results of Peterson and Barney's (1952) study of formant frequencies F_1 and F_2 for vowels spoken by 76 different speakers. (Note that the F_1 axis is a logarithmic scale. 1 kHz = 1000 Hz.)

Figure 6 contain about 90 per cent of the data points obtained in each phonetic category. Some of the data points for each phonetic category 'spilled out' into other vowel loops; and you will also note that some of the loops overlap. Thus, we can see that there is quite a lot of variation from speaker to speaker in the acoustic properties of vowels.

This variation should not be surprising, however, in light of what we said earlier about the relation between the properties of the vocal tract and the sounds it produces. Remember that the acoustic properties of speech sounds are determined by the length and shape of the vocal tract. Just as people come in different sizes and shapes, so do vocal tracts; thus, we should not be surprised to find that similar articulatory gestures will produce different acoustic patterns in different-sized vocal tracts. The frequency of the first formant (F_1) for the vowel [a], for example, varies from 730 Hz in adult men to 1030 Hz in children in Peterson and Barney's data. This is apparently because adult men have longer vocal tracts than children. (Frequency is inversely related to length of a resonating chamber – remember our bottle example.) The shape of the formant transitions associated with the production of different consonants also changes as a function of vocal tract size. It appears, therefore, that listeners must somehow make a judgement about the size of a speaker's vocal tract before they can identify the sounds in a speech signal correctly.

Now, how in the world can listeners do this? It isn't by looking at the speaker and sizing up her/his vocal tract because we have no trouble at all in understanding the speech of people whom we can't see and whom we haven't seen before, for example, strangers on the telephone. The Ladefoged and Broadbent experiment indicates that listeners can apparently make use of the formant frequency range in a short bit of speech (the introductory sentence in the experiment) to make an estimate of the size of a speaker's vocal tract. (Of course this is an unconscious judgement; we have no evidence that listeners have any conscious knowledge of the length of a speaker's vocal tract.) But more recent experiments by Darwin (1971) and Rand (1971) indicate that listeners do not have to wait to hear a one- to three-second bit of speech before they can begin to identify the sounds in a speech signal. It appears that certain vowels can be used by listeners to identify instantly the size of the vocal tract that they are listening to.

In an experiment on vowel identification Peterson and Barney (1952) found that listeners had no trouble identifying the vowels [i] and [u] pronounced by many different speakers. That is, listeners in the experiment classified the vowels [i] and [u] with great consistency. The vowel [a] was also consistently identified, but less so than [i] or [u], perhaps because of dialect variation. Other vowels such as [ɛ], [æ], [e] and [ɪ] were not consistently identified; that is, the listeners did not agree on what vowel they thought they heard. Thus, there seems to be something special about the vowels [i] and [u].

Stevens and House (1955) showed that these vowels, [i] and [u], are **determinate** – a particular formant pattern for these vowels can only be produced by a vocal tract of a particular size. Stevens and House also showed that these vowels are acoustically stable and that fairly large errors in tongue placement in the articulation of these vowels can occur without disturbing the stable acoustic pattern of these vowels. A listener could use these vowels to arrive instantly at an estimate of the size of the vocal tract that produced these sounds. Gerstman (1967) has shown that a computer program can be written which can derive a speaker's 'vowel space' by using the formant frequencies of the vowel [i] or [u].

Take a look at Figure 6 again. You will notice that the vowels are arranged in a sort of triangle. The vowels [i] and [u], along with [a], essentially define the limits of the 'vowel space' – each of these vowels sits on a vertex of the triangle. For this reason these vowels are sometimes referred to as the **point vowels**. The other vowels are fairly evenly distributed between the point vowels. Lieberman (1975) has pointed out that this appears to be a general principle. A language with only three vowels will have [i], [a] and [u]. A five-vowel language will partition the vowel space by having a vowel between [i] and [a] and another between [a] and [u]. The determinate vowels thus form the boundaries of the vowel space, and they appear to enable a listener to map out a speaker's vowel space.

Other sounds may also give a listener information about the size of a speaker's vocal tract – the fricative [s], for example; but vowels like [i] and [u] appear to be the best 'vocal tract calibrating signals'. These determinate vowels are extremely useful sounds. They are acoustically stable, and they serve as extremely efficient vocal tract calibrating signals. It is not surprising, therefore, that these sounds appear to be highly valued and that, as far as we know, they appear in all of the languages in the world. It also should not be surprising that the human vocal tract seems to have evolved so that these vowels can be accurately produced even with a certain amount of articulatory sloppiness, thus ensuring rapid and efficient communication through speech (Lieberman, 1973, 1975).

'Invariants' in Speech Perception

We have tended to dwell primarily on the *lack* of invariant cues for speech perception. We need not go so far as to say that there are no invariant acoustic cues for speech perception, but we have tried to point out that there simply do not appear to be enough invariant acoustic cues to base a theory on. We will briefly mention a couple of areas in which some invariant cues seem to have been found and then move on to summarize our observations on speech perception.

Perhaps the most famous 'invariant' has been found in extensive research on the voiced/unvoiced distinction in stop consonants. Lisker and Abramson (1964) investigated the acoustic cue of **voice onset time** (the difference between the onset of F_1 and F_2 mentioned above) in a great many languages. Voice onset time is an acoustic measure of the difference – or lack of one – between the time of the release of oral closure for stop consonants and the beginning of vocal cord vibration (voicing). This speech cue appears in many languages. In English, for example, a bilabial stop is heard as a [p] if voicing is delayed for about 40 msec.; but a [b] is heard if there is less than a 40 msec. delay in voicing. The 40 msec. delay mark seems to be the perceptual boundary between [p] and [b]; the boundary is at the same place for other stop consonants as well. Interestingly enough, when subjects are asked to listen for differences between speech sounds that vary in terms of voice onset time, they are very good at hearing the difference between sounds on opposite sides of the 40 msec. boundary; but they find it difficult or impossible to hear a difference between sounds that lie on the same side of the boundary. That is, two bilabial stops with 30 msec. and 50 msec. voice onset lags will be heard as different (the first as a [b], the second as a [p]); but two bilabial stops with, say, 10 msec. and 30 msec. voice onset lags do not sound different (they are both heard as [b]s, even though they are the same distance apart in terms of voice onset lag as the sounds in our first example). This phenomenon is known as '**categorical perception**' – the sounds are heard as different only if they come from different 'categories'. Eimas *et al.* (1971) have shown that four-week-old infants display the same sort of bias.

Cutting and Rosner (1974) have also observed a similar sort of categorical perception in the discrimination of fricatives from affricates, e.g., [ʃ] and [tʃ], as in *shop* vs *chop*. Here, the distinction seems to be based on differences in 'rise time', i.e., the time it takes for the acoustic signal to reach maximum intensity. For the [ʃ] sound the rise time is relatively long, whereas for a [tʃ] the maximum intensity is reached rather quickly. Discrimination experiments show that there is a definite categorical boundary between [ʃ] and [tʃ] when rise time is systematically varied. There are other cues that signal the fricative/affricate distinction, too (see Repp *et al.*, 1978).

Thus, as we said before, it's not the case that there are no acoustic invariants. It's just that there don't seem to be enough of them; and, as Mattingly (1976) has pointed out, it may even be that some of the 'invariants' themselves sometimes vary. We simply cannot cut up the speech signal into the discrete sound segments that speakers believe they produce and listeners believe they hear. This has led many (Liberman *et al.*, 1967; Liberman and Studdert-Kennedy, 1979; Lieberman, 1973, 1975) to believe that speakers and hearers deal not in acoustic invariants but in articulatory events that are encoded in the speech signal by certain cues or constellations of cues. Thus, differences between the consonants [b], [d] and [g], for example, are signalled by acoustically recognizable changes in the sounds produced by the vocal tract. The sound changes reflect both the oral closure associated with stop consonant articulation and also where in the vocal tract the closure is made. Listeners, apparently by using some sort of tacit knowledge about the way vocal tracts work, somehow actively reconstruct the sequence of articulatory events that produced the sounds they hear. Thus, we must assume that listeners know something about the acoustic results of articulatory manoeuvres, and we must also assume that they are able to 'calibrate' their perceptions for particular vocal tracts.

A note on learning. If this theory is, in fact, correct, how do children, new to the world of speech, manage to get useful linguistic information from the outputs of vocal tracts which differ from one another and which also differ greatly from children's own vocal tracts in size, shape and acoustical properties? That is, how do children learn what they need to know about vocal tracts in order to process speech sounds? Fant (1953) suggested that it might be reasonable to suppose that children accomplish this by 'studying' their own vocal tracts, perhaps through vocal play like babbling; he pointed out that they could then apply what would amount to a simple mathematical transformation to the information they had gained which would enable them to process speech sounds. The idea is that children find out what sorts of articulatory gestures produce what sorts of sounds in their own vocal tracts and then somehow extrapolate what they have found out about the acoustic properties of their own vocal tracts to other vocal tracts. There are, however, all sorts of difficulties with this view. To begin with, it doesn't look as if one needs to have a functional vocal tract to be able to learn to understand speech. Lenneberg (1967) described a number of medical cases involving people with extensive congenital damage to the vocal tract who were physiologically incapable of speaking from birth but who, nevertheless, had no trouble learning to understand speech. Thus, one need not have had first-hand experience with one's own vocal tract in order to be able to learn to understand speech.

A further problem we encounter with this is that a child's vocal tract is simply not just a smaller version of an adult's; the vocal tracts of children differ from those of adults not only in size but also in shape and acoustical properties (Lieberman *et al.*, 1972; Stark, 1979). No simple mathematical transformation would suffice to relate the properties of children's vocal tracts to those of adults. Add to this the fact that children's vocal tracts change quite rapidly and drastically during the first three years of life, and it starts to seem more likely that children's vocal tracts might be more of a problem than a help for them. Children must be able to determine how their vocal tracts work before they can produce speech; Mattingly (1976) has suggested that one of the functions of the so-called 'babbling' stage in speech development might be to help children become familiar with their vocal tracts and, in some sense, enable children to 'map out' their vocal tracts. Since children apparently use data they get from adult vocal tracts in learning to produce speech with their own vocal tracts, we run into many problems. As we have noted, not only are children's vocal tracts very different from adults', they are also changing in size and shape at a fairly rapid rate during language development. It looks as if we might be forced to say that children must understand something about both adult and child vocal tracts, and also something about how vocal tracts change during physiological maturation. We might have to assume, then, that children come into the world equipped with the mechanisms necessary for them to 'crack the code' of speech. We really have only the faintest idea about what those mechanisms might be; and, in fact, we don't have very many good ideas about how to find out more. It appears that we must look to the future for more information on the actual mechanisms that are involved in speech perception and its development.

Redundancy

In our discussion of speech perception we have focused on what we might call the 'limiting condition' for speech perception. We have focused on situations in which the only information available to listeners is the information contained in the acoustic shape of speech sounds. We have been focusing, therefore, on a somewhat unnatural condition. We would like to point out that the perception of individual speech sounds is demonstrably sensitive to decisions at what we might call the 'higher' levels of speech analysis. A large number of studies have shown that the intelligibility of a speech signal is related to its redundancy. The decisions that listeners make about the phonetic content of a bit of speech are sensitive to what they know – or think they know – about the lexical, syntactic and semantic analysis of the speech signal. In fact, as we shall see later on, it seems plausible to assume that decisions at every level of analysis affect decisions at other levels, both 'higher' and 'lower'. That is, there is both feed-back and feed-forward at all levels of linguistic analysis. The analysis that listeners finally arrive at is, thus, the 'best fit' analysis, given all the information that is available to listeners about the acoustic wave form, the situation in which the sounds were uttered, etc.

The classic experiments in this area involve investigations of the intelligibility of speech heard under 'noisy' conditions. Subjects listen to speech in situations very much like those we encounter in listening to a weak radio signal or a poor telephone connection in which there is a lot of 'static' in the background. (See Miller, Heise and Lichten, 1951, for example.) It has been found that actual words can be correctly understood at considerably higher noise levels (i.e., when there is more static) than nonsense words. We presume that this is because listeners can use what they know about the actual shapes of actual words to, in some sense, 'fill in the gaps' when information is lost due to the noise in the signal. Words in sentences can be correctly identified at even higher levels of noise than words that are simply presented in unstructured lists. And, listeners seem to tolerate still higher levels of noise in the recognition of words in sentences that are put together in connected discourse. Thus, it appears that more organization in the speech signal enables listeners to tolerate more noise in the signal. Apparently, increased structure in the speech signal at all levels enables listeners to rely less heavily on a fine-grained analysis of the acoustic characteristics of the signal. It is also very likely that certain *non*linguistic variables affect intelligibility: knowledge of the speech situation, the topic of conversation, etc., clearly seem to help listeners comprehend a speech signal. Thus, in the real world, the process of speech perception does not seem to involve the filtering out of irrelevant information but rather the adding of information which can be used properly to decode the speech signal. The phonetic analysis of a speech signal involves the integration of acoustic information with other information that is available to the listener. Listeners actively compute the phonetic content of a message by using all sorts of background knowledge. Thus, it is not only listeners' expectations of certain sound patterns that influence what they hear but also their expectations of semantic, syntactic and discourse patterns.

Producing Speech Sounds

We have already said quite a bit about how speech sounds are produced in the preceding sections, so we won't have much more to say in this section. Our focus here will be on the processes that are involved in planning an utterance.

Planning speech. One of the main points of our discussion of speech perception was that a simple beads-on-a-string model for speech perception could not work. Our main point here will be that a beads-on-a-string model for speech production cannot work either. Because the vocal tract is not inertia-free and cannot change from one position to another instantaneously, and because of the different lengths and conduction rates of the nerves that control the vocal apparatus, it appears that the instructions to the vocal tract must be 'scrambled' so that the right articulatory gestures happen at the right time. That is, the instructions to the articulators cannot be sent out in an order that strictly follows the order in which phonetic segments appear in a phonetic representation.

Consider our *slip/sloop* example from the discussion above. We noted that (for most speakers) the onset of rounding for the [u] sound in *sloop* occurs at the beginning of the word. In this case the character of the [s] is being determined in part by a feature of a sound segment that is two segments away from the [s] in the phonetic representation. The vocal tract instructor must plan ahead so that the required amount of rounding is achieved by the time the [u] is reached. Thus, the vocal tract instructor must anticipate certain sounds that are coming up in a word and initiate certain articulatory gestures early so that the desired combination of articulatory gestures occurs at the right time.

Lenneberg (1967) has pointed out that it is not just inertia in the vocal tract that requires the vocal tract instructor to plan ahead. The various articulators are different distances away from the brain centres which appear to control the articulation of speech. It looks as if certain nerve impulses must be sent out before others because it takes longer for nerve impulses to reach some articulators than others. Thus, we have reason to suspect that what we might call the 'neuronal firing order' is different from the order in which the actual movements of the articulators take place. A particularly dramatic example of this comes from the work of Krmpotić (cited in Lenneberg, 1967). Krmpotić was interested in the problems posed by differences in conduction times for the various nerves that control the speech apparatus, and he studied the anatomy of these nerves and computed the so-called 'neuromuscular indexes' for all of the major muscles involved in speech production. The details of all this need not concern us here, but this study of the anatomy of the nerves shows that it may easily take up to 30 msec. longer for nerve impulses to reach the muscles that control the larynx than it does for nerve impulses to reach muscles in and around the oral cavity. Therefore, the production of a syllable like [ba], where we have simultaneous lip closure and vocal cord vibration, requires that the instruction to the vocal cords in the larynx be sent out earlier than the instruction to the lips (about 30 msec. earlier, if Krmpotić's calculations are correct).

It's clear, then, that there must be quite a bit of precision timing involved in speech production if all of the various articulators are to be coordinated. It's not surprising, then, that we encounter patients with brain damage (e.g., stroke patients) who have difficulties in keeping speech sounds in the right order. Patients who have this sort of problem speak very slowly and appear to have to concentrate very hard when they are speaking – as if they have to think consciously about keeping the sounds in the right order. They constantly mix up sounds despite all this apparent effort: *is* may come out as *si*, *task* as *taks*, etc. These patients often have trouble getting words out in the correct order, too. Such patients are fully aware of their difficulties and can often make a fresh start and repeat their utterances again without errors. However, in severe cases, the 'corrected' utterance may contain new mistakes.

The problem of serial ordering in speech. Sequencing errors like these can also be found in everyday – i.e., nonpathological – speech. Examples of these 'slips of the tongue', as they are called, are not hard to find if you listen carefully to the speech of others. Many linguists and psycholinguists (e.g., Fromkin, 1971; Garrett, 1975, 1976) have pointed out the regularities that can be found in such errors and have noted that the units that are changed or moved in such errors correspond quite well to the units proposed by linguists in their grammars: phones, morphemes, words, etc. These data have been used to argue that these units are the planning units for speech production.

Such studies – and we shall refer to them again in later chapters – use speech error data to test predictions that are based on linguistic theory. Others, most notably Karl Lashley (1951; see also Garrett, 1975, 1976; and Shattuck-Hufnagel, 1980), have used such error data in a different

56

way. Lashley argued that exchange errors such as those below reveal important things about the speaking process. Errors (taken from Shattuck-Hufnagel, 1980) such as

A *street* on Eddy *house*   (house on Eddy street)
They put their *lips*
through their *teeth*   (teeth through their lips)
There's no word *in* it
for English   (for it in English)

indicate that speakers must have some sort of representation of a sentence that spans more than just the next word or phoneme of the utterance. Otherwise, we could not explain how a word from later in an utterance could appear earlier than it was supposed to. This is significant because it shows that word-by-word, stimulus-response models, e.g., the response-chain model of Skinner (1938) and other so-called 'radical behaviourists', are not adequate because they cannot predict such errors.

For the radical behaviourists, serial ordering in any behaviour is a consequence of **response chaining**; that is, the production of each response in a **behaviour chain** serves as the stimulus for the next response. Radical behaviourists like Skinner explicitly state that a behaviour chain has no structure or organization beyond that contained in the associative connections between the elementary units that make up the chain. Thus, serial order in language is a consequence of (learned) associations between elementary linguistic units – presumably words or individual sounds. A sentence, then, is to be viewed as a behaviour chain, each element of which provides the stimulus for the production of the succeeding element. A sentence is produced by the speaker word by word: the speaker produces a word, that word provides the stimulus for the production of another word, and so on until a complete utterance is produced.

Lashley (1951) pointed out that such associative chain models cannot predict or explain exchange errors like the ones above because in these cases the character of earlier portions of the utterance is, in some sense, determined by the intended character of later portions of the utterance. It appears that speech is planned beforehand in sequences that are longer than single linguistic elements. There must be some sort of 'planning level' at which a significant part of an utterance – if not the utterance as a whole – is represented. If this were not the case we would not be able to get things mixed up in uttering a sentence or phrase. To put it simply, the fact that such speech errors occur indicates that our plans for utterances can sometimes go awry, and this presupposes that we plan our utterances before we start to utter them. We don't simply start a chain of associations going, we plan ahead and know where we are going before we start to speak.

You can easily demonstrate the inadequacy of associative chain models by carrying out a simple experiment. You need a group of people, four or five is a good number, although more is even better. Take a piece of paper and write a word at the top of it. Pass this paper to another person and have him/her write down, under your word, the first word that pops into her/his head after reading your word. This person then folds the paper over so that only the word he or she wrote shows and passes it on to the next person, who reads the word and writes down the first word that pops into her/his head and then folds the paper so that only her/his word shows before passing it on to another person. Keep this up for a while and then unfold the paper and see what you get. Odds are that it won't even resemble a sentence. You may, however, produce something that looks like Dadaist poetry.

Summary

We have seen, then, that speaking involves quite a bit of complex planning. The experimental evidence indicates that the 'vocal tract instructor' must plan ahead, taking into account such things as the different amounts of time it takes for neural messages to reach the muscles that control the articulators, and the amount of time it takes the various articulators to assume various positions. We have very little notion about how this complex integration is accomplished, we simply know that somehow or other it is accomplished. We also know that speakers appear to plan their sentences before they utter them, and we have argued that this makes a simple, response-chaining model for speech production seem unlikely.

In our discussion of speech perception we have pointed out the disappointing lack of invariant cues for the recognition of speech sounds. The beads-on-a-string model, appealing as it is, appears to be the wrong model for speech perception. Listeners, first of all, must be able to 'tune' their perceptions for different speakers. We have suggested that they may be able to do this by noting the acoustic shape that the vowels [i] and [u] take on in different speakers' speech. We also pointed out that listeners appear to decode the speech signal in terms of syllable-sized units, and that they do this by somehow figuring out what sorts of articulatory movements would have produced the sounds that they hear. It appears that speech perception is not a matter of passively sitting by and waiting for specific cues to turn up, but, rather, that it is a matter of actively reconstructing a speaker's message on the basis of a wide range of acoustic and, it seems, probably nonacoustic information.

We have not answered the question, 'How do we produce and understand speech sounds?' What we hope we have done, however, is to suggest what kinds of answers seem most likely. The search for adequate and worked-out models goes on.

4. *The Connection between Grammar and Speech*

What do we do when we hear sentences? This question seems prudently academic: sentences are so small and specific that they would appear to have little to do with life's larger concerns. Yet, when we look closely we find that this apparently simple question leads us to consider all sorts of deep questions about people, about their minds, and about human biology. Every minute, we put ideas into sentences and, somewhat imperfectly, let words carry our thoughts. The ways in which we put thoughts into words and get thoughts out of the words of others involve subtle and imperfectly understood principles of human psychology. We shall try to glimpse these principles by looking at the mechanisms of syntax. However, given the apparent complexity of the problems involved, we cannot expect complete answers right now.

The Mind, its Principles, and Time

Science often advances by finding principles of great generality in small observations, and we will try to present our observations in the same way. Our goal is not to 'describe' language processes or to prove truths about them. Instead, we will attempt to illustrate general principles of the mind at work.

Consider the sentence below. (It is, indeed, a sentence, by the way.)

The man who hunts ducks out on weekends.

The first thing that you will notice is that this sentence is irritating. It takes several readings for most people to understand this sentence. In fact, it may take several readings to recognize that it *is* a sentence. The problem seems to lie in the middle. A pause after *hunts* could make things clearer. In order to understand the sentence we must realize that the verb *hunts* has no direct object and that the word *ducks*, which would fit in very nicely as the direct object of *hunts*, must be regarded as a verb (the main verb of the sentence, in fact).

How did we go wrong? It appears that we were somewhat impatient. If we had waited until we had read the whole sentence before deciding if *ducks* was a noun or a verb we would not have run into trouble. That is, we could have avoided problems by waiting and not jumping to hasty conclusions. The fact is, though, that we don't seem to be able to avoid this kind of impatience. We don't seem to want to take the *time* to 'do things right' in this sentence. This is part of the point we are trying to make here: the processing of sentences takes time, though not much time. One reason we can understand sentences so rapidly is that we make decisions about the structure of a sentence before we have heard (or read) the whole sentence. Such 'snap judgements' serve us very well in most situations; but occasionally, as we have seen, they lead us down the garden path. We might also go a little further and note that it may very well be that this not only helps us to understand rapidly but also makes it possible for us to understand sentences at all. After all, when we are listening to someone speak, that person's words don't hang around in the air like words on a printed page – they disappear as soon as they are uttered. We don't have the luxury of being able to sit back and scan the words in a spoken sentence, as we can if it is in written form. Even if we could remember all the words in a sentence without making some guesses about how they relate to one another, we still could not afford the time involved in waiting until the end of the sentence. We might miss something important at the beginning of the speaker's next sentence. Words and sentences come thick and fast in normal spoken speech, and we must deal with them quickly and efficiently if we are to get the speaker's message without missing anything.

It is this fact, that time is involved, that distinguishes the study of sentence perception from the study of grammar itself. Grammars, as we shall see, exist, in a sense, outside of time. Grammars describe the relations between parts of sentences, but they do not reveal how we use parts of a sentence to predict other parts. The challenge that confronts us in building a theory of sentence perception is to describe the relation between the nontemporal concept of grammar and its use in time.

We assume that speakers and hearers actually use their knowledge of grammar in split-second unconscious reasoning, and we will attempt to present evidence for this assumption. That is, we assume that a grammar is a real part of the psychological equipment that we use to understand and produce speech. We might look upon a grammar as a kind of mental map: you can see the whole thing at once, and you can also use it to guide your travels (in time). Speakers may use this information in one way, and hearers in another.

Now, how much time are we talking about? Not much, it appears. A very rough estimate is that it takes us about two seconds to understand an average sentence, from the time the speaker starts uttering it until we get the message a little bit after the sentence has been uttered. It is extremely difficult for us to introspect consciously about what we do when we understand sentences. The comprehension process seems to proceed automatically and at some unconscious level. It appears that sentence comprehension is as far beyond conscious introspection as is trying to think about how each muscle in our legs works while we are running. We need to go about studying sentence comprehension through indirect means in scientific experiments. We will need to consider what sophisticated experimental studies reveal about how we understand sentences, in addition to our conscious ruminations about sentences and what makes them easy or difficult to understand.

Using Incomplete Information

Our example sentence, *The man who hunts ducks out on weekends*, reveals another fundamental aspect of sentence perception: we make decisions on the basis of *incomplete information*. The hearer has decided to treat *ducks* as the direct object of *hunts* before he or she has reached the end of the sentence. The irritating difficulty with this sentence lies in the undoing of the mistake. But it is not only the word *ducks* that could lead us astray. Both *hunt* and *man* can also be either nouns or verbs (e.g., *a fox hunt, to man a ship*). These words do not cause us difficulties, though, because their prior contexts give us information about their parts of speech. *Man* is preceded by the article *the*, which always comes before a noun. The pronoun *who* precedes *hunts*, which suggests that it is a verb. We have used the weaker term *suggests* here because *who* does not always come before a verb. We can construct phrases like

The man who (fox) hunts always thrill

where the opposite reading is forced. *Hunts* is a plural noun here. Problems arise in our example sentence because *subsequent* context is needed to make the correct decisions about how to treat the word *ducks*. The word has a prior context that favours a noun reading, while the subsequent context must eventually overrule the prior context in favour of a verb reading.

We have now established that there is a left-to-right

asymmetry in sentence comprehension. It is easier to select one of two possible analyses on the basis of prior context than it is to make decisions on the basis of subsequent context. This distinction is unavailable if we look at the grammar alone, since grammars cannot express what happens during the actual process of sentence perception.

Syntactic Expectation

As we noted above, our knowledge of words includes hidden knowledge about the structure that they enter into. This structure is closely linked to, but not identified with, meaning. Suppose that you heard a sentence that began *John craned.* You would immediately know that it was incomplete and, moreover, that it would probably be followed by *his neck.* The verb *crane* occurs only with the noun *neck*, although we might have variation in the possessive pronoun, *his*, *her* or *its*, depending on what the subject of *crane* is.

Other words have features of meaning that dictate subsequent structure. Thus, the verb *put* in *John put the book* requires something more. We know this is incomplete, and we know something about what is missing: an indication of *location*. We have advance knowledge of what to expect, but we do not know exactly in what grammatical form the location will appear. It could be as a particle (*He put the book down*), as a prepositional phrase (*He put the book on the table*), or as an adverb (*He put the book here*). Not every reference to location will work. If we say **He put the book table* (*=ungrammatical) we have used a locative word (*table*) and satisfied the purely meaning (or semantic) requirements of the verb *put*; but we have failed to honour the structural requirements of the verb *put*, namely, that location be expressed by prepositional phrase, particle or adverb. We can summarize our discussion by saying that certain verbs, when encountered, carry or *propose* a small set of alternatives, one of which *must* be realized. The mind thus primes itself for what is coming.

There are two important observations to be made about lexical contributions to structure. The first is that verbs, as we have seen, appear to play a dominant role. They organize the sentence. Until the verb appears, a very large set of alternatives exists. As an exercise, imagine all of the different phrases that could follow the expression *the man*. This phrase could be followed by all sorts of different types of words: *can, since, he, who, that, Bill, and, of, five* etc. Once you have said *the man*, the next word could be just about any part of speech, including an article. For instance, *the man the girl saw coming.* When the verb arrives, a large set of alternatives remains, but certain verb-requirements must be met, or we know something is missing.

A second observation involves the same problem of predicting what comes next. Everyone has the feeling or intuition that a language has some 'basic order'. We talk about languages as being 'verb-final' or putting adjectives after nouns. There is truth in these intuitions, but the facts persistently appear to defy some of these intuitions. There simply cannot be any absolute statement of order in English. Let's consider a few more examples until this claim becomes clear. Adjectives seem to be fixed in where they can occur. A natural observation is that adjectives occur before nouns (*the big man*) and not after them (**the man big*). However, when two adjectives are involved, it is perfectly acceptable for them to follow a noun: *the man big and strong.* Now let's try the claim that articles never appear after adjectives: **big the man.* This is also not true because we find sequences like *however big the man is.* Nor is it the case that adjectives always modify the nouns next to which they appear: *He sat down next to the rock tired* means that *he* and not the *rock* is tired. These examples could be extended to cover every seemingly absolute order of phrases to be found in English.

These observations might lead us to the simple claim that there is no order at all for English. Now, however, we have erred in the other direction. After all, *house blue the see did I* seems very ungrammatical, although when it is read backwards it is perfectly meaningful and grammatical. Order doesn't exist, and yet it does. We have a paradox. Science often moves forward by the recognition of, and eventual resolution of, paradoxes. Usually a more sophisticated approach is needed to dissolve the paradox. This is what happened in linguistics.

Order and Structure in Sentences

In a highly simplified fashion we are reconstructing the history of linguistics. Decades of work went into intricate attempts to articulate the order of grammatical elements in English. These efforts were revolutionized in the late 1950s when Noam Chomsky (1957) introduced the notion of **transformational rules** that allowed a sentence to have two structures and two orders simultaneously. The first structure, known as the **deep structure**, provides a simple ordering of subject, verb, object etc. The second structure, known as the **surface structure**, is the result of the operation of rules which change the initial deep structure. The idea is that one order is basic, and all acceptable alternative orders are systematic deviations from this basic order. The system in the deviations can be described by rules.

Chomsky's system has come to be regarded as one of the intellectual landmarks of the twentieth century. His system, though quite abstract, has a certain amount of intuitive immediacy. What did he do? He gave a natural explanation for sentences like the one we just used. The deep structure of

What did he do?

is

He did do what?

A transformation, which we could call **question formation**, moves the *what* to the front of the sentence. (Another rule will invert *he* and *did* to derive *What did he do?* from *What he did do?*) The transformation captures our intuition that the *what* is really the object of the verb. Current versions of transformational grammar in fact claim that an invisible **trace** is left in the object position: *What did he do (trace)?* (The traces can, in fact, become 'audible' in some sentences because some phonological rules are sensitive to their presence, see Radford, 1981.)

Time and Grammar

We have now introduced two different kinds of descriptions. On the one hand, we have seen that the hearer moves 'left-to-right' through a sentence, making proposals about the structure that is to follow. On the other hand, we have seen that the grammatical concept of 'transformation' can resolve the problem of the variety of orders in which sentences can come. We are now in a position to ask a question that we shall reconsider several times: How do these two systems (the sentence processor and the grammar) interact?

A reasonable hypothesis is that hearers use transformations in order to make proposals about what will follow in a sentence. It is far from clear *how* they use transformations. Transformations are not described in terms of time: they refer to a whole sentence at once. (In fact, the technical definition of a transformation is a rule which maps one whole structure (sentence) into another.) In our example we said that the *what* was moved from object position to the front of the sentence. The hearer will know that the *what* has probably been moved as soon as he or she hears it, but he or she will not know where it came from.

For instance, a hearer can make some decisions when he or she hears just *what* at the beginning of a sentence. The range of possibilities is not unlimited: subject (*What's cooking?*), object (*What did you cook?*), or object of a preposition (*What did you cook the fish in?*). The hearer can summon these alternatives and then allow later words to weed out the incorrect ones. He or she might alternatively make a decision in advance (e.g., *what* = object, as is often the case) and then revise that decision when evidence to the contrary appears. Technically, both of these decisions represent partial uses of the grammar. In each case a syntactic decision comes in two parts. Until one knows exactly where the *what* belongs, there remains a potentially large number of possibilities. If a person could not make partial use of the grammar, he could not understand a part of a sentence until he had heard the whole sentence.

In general, the hearer needs some auxiliary equipment to make the translation from a grammar to what we might call a time-sensitive parser. A **parser** assigns a syntactic function to words as we hear them. The parser must have the capacity both to propose or predict structure and to delay making final decisions about structure because of the incomplete nature of the information available to it at any given point in a sentence. It needs a kind of *delayer*. The nontemporal grammar has no capacity to include a delay mechanism because the grammar is outside of time. Therefore we shall have to invent one as an auxiliary to the grammar.

The specific mechanisms of perception – as far as we understand them – will be the topic of close attention in the pages to come. What we have described thus far is an introduction to the major issues. To summarize, we have made the following important points:

1. We must distinguish carefully between a *grammar* – a person's knowledge of the structure of his or her language – and *sentence perception* – how people actually comprehend sentences. A grammar is abstract and timeless, whereas sentence perception takes place in real time.
2. Sentence perception makes use of the grammar in its unconscious reasoning. We therefore need to examine how these two aspects of language interact.
3. In sentence perception, we make decisions about what we hear on the basis of incomplete information. Since what we hear occurs in real time, we make more use of prior context in our decisions than of subsequent context. Sentences in which the subsequent context forces us to change our earlier decisions are more difficult to comprehend.
4. Our decisions about sentence meaning are based on our knowledge of the structure of sentences, and, in particular, the constructions associated with verbs.
5. A critical problem is that there seems to be an enormous variety of possible word orders in English; so how do speakers cope? One way out of this problem is to suppose that there is a basic word order from which all other orders are systematically derived. This is essentially the solution proposed by Chomsky. It is possible that hearers make use of some similar mechanism when they comprehend speech. In other words, they may relate an altered word order to a more basic one in order to comprehend a sentence. We may therefore envisage every sentence as having two levels, a deep basic one, and a surface actual one. Operations called *transformations* link one with the other.

70

Mental Abstractions

A theory of language that postulates the existence of two levels of representation for every sentence (deep and surface structures) makes some strong statements about the nature of the mind. One of these levels – deep structure – is not manifested in the spoken string of words. It must be inferred. The fact that the structures and the transformations are not themselves readily observable means that fundamental aspects of language are *abstract*. It was this shift in modern linguistics toward the discussion of abstractions that caused changes in psycholinguistics. Instead of studying speech *per se* we have turned to the study of the abstract language within speech. Ultimately, many mysteries about speech – which can be defined simply as spoken output – can be solved by taking a deeper perspective.

There are many other aspects of the mind that enter language which we have given short shrift. We shall not do them justice, but they are important nonetheless. Ideas, of course, are poured into words. In addition, our language also reflects our mood, personality and state of health. Tiny perturbations of the speech stream can suggest to a listener that the speaker is angry, insincere, insane, eager, unwell, or a host of other subtle attitudes and emotions. How such diverse factors are rapidly integrated defies any known theory of cognitive psychology. Our efforts to build mechanisms in this direction constitute, therefore, a few steps toward a theory of cognitive psychology.

Psychological Infinities

The notion of grammar that we have developed is both infinite and limited, which is an apparent paradox. This double characteristic is what makes it possible to represent an infinite system within a finite mind. The mind, we presume, is realized somehow in the brain; and the brain must be finite because it fits into the human head, which, by simple observation, is itself finite (i.e., it fits into a certain space).

What, then, do we mean by 'infinite'? We shall give progressively more technical definitions. The grammar of English will allow us to produce an infinitely long sentence: we could say, *John, who begat Sidney, who begat Fred, who begat Harry, who* . . . . We could continue on forever if we could live forever. The system has infinite potential, but the people who use it do not. Therefore, the fact that no infinite sentence will ever be uttered results from a limitation that is essentially external to the system: human mortality.

We shall look at three kinds of infinite potential in language. We can use **conjunction** to repeat the same operation over and over and over and over and over, and . . . here, clearly, we have an example of one of them. We can also 'loop' to construct endless strings of adjectives, *a big, big, big, big, big, big, big, big house.* A third kind involves **compounds**: *elephant hide wallet dealer network, convention report statistics.*

Other kinds of infinities are excluded: we cannot put together an infinite string of articles, for example, as in *the, a, the, a, the.* There is no way that such a sequence could occur in any English sentence. (Except, of course, as part of a sentence like the one you just read.) Such kinds of sequences do not occur in any other known language either. Other languages duplicate, with some minor variations, just those kinds of infinities that we can find in English. If we see language as purely the product of culture and social circumstances, then this uniformity is quite amazing. But, if we see language as a product of our biological nature, then uniformity across languages is no more surprising than the observation that people in all cultures have two eyes and one nose. For this reason we say that the common features in the languages of the world are **linguistic universals**.

Now we may examine the notion of incomplete information from another perspective. There is no doubt that hearers all ultimately receive sufficient information about the meanings of sentences they hear to converse satisfactorily. What we have been arguing, in effect, is that there are two sources of information, one external and one internal (see Chapter 3). Part of the information comes from the speaker in the form of speech. The external information is designed to fit the internal information provided by the hearer through the common biological design he shares with all humans. In other words, our genetic structure contains information about the structure of language which we can use to enhance or build upon what we hear. There is much controversy over what must be genetically given, but whatever is universal does not need to be conveyed because it is mutually possessed.

Note, by the way, that language is not the only domain in which the mind has infinite potential. We can in principle continue the sequence of integers 1, 2, 3, 4, 5 . . . forever. The term *in principle* refers once again to the extraneous factors which prevent this potential from being realized. We would get hungry, die, or become bored before getting to infinity. But we would not want to build into a description of a mathematical system the possibility of the death or loss of interest of the counter. Our minds, if not our bodies, have a boundless, infinite potential. Not to see this feature of the mind is to miss its essence. It is surprising to realize that centuries of contemplation of the nature of humanity went by before this simple truth became clear.

Linguistic and mathematical infinities differ, though, in their mental status. We process linguistic infinities on a virtually instantaneous basis, while mathematical notions of infinity usually require much thought, not to mention a fair amount of explicit instruction, as in calculus and the theory of limits. Little work has been done on the psychology of mathematics, but it may be fundamentally different from the psychology of language. Understanding sentences appears to be something that 'comes naturally'; understanding a proof in algebraic topology takes a lot of work and requires a lot of explicit instruction. Distinctions like these, however, are rather crude and often dissolve upon closer scrutiny. These questions are topics of current research; but we leave this topic with a simple suggestion: mathematical and linguistic abilities are psychologically different.

Creativity and Humanity

In popular vocabulary the word 'mechanical' is often taken to be the opposite of 'creative'. At first sight, our discussion may seem perverse because we shall claim that human abilities are both creative and mechanical. But, as we shall try to explain, recent thinking suggests that this claim is a reasonable one.

Much of the tension between 'scientific' and 'humanistic' perspectives of the human being can be traced to the fact that humanists have felt that scientists reduce human beings to something less than they are. The Darwinian revolution has the persistent implication that human beings are not very different from monkeys. Neurological and psychological research threatens to reduce the grandeur of human emotion to the mechanics of chemistry or habit formation.

Scientists, on the other hand, have regarded the claims of humanists as little more than quaint and sentimental, but illusory, assertions about the special value of the human spirit. The revolution in linguistics may allow us to develop a concept of the human being which combines the scientific rigour of mechanical models with the humanistic respect for creativity, unpredictability and our commitment to abstract or spiritual values.

How can this synthesis be achieved? The crucial step is this: make a machine that has creativity built into it. Every sentence has a similar pattern; this part seems mechanical. And yet every sentence is slightly different because it uses different words, in slightly different orders, with slightly different emphases, etc. Many of the sentences we utter have never been uttered before by any human in the history of mankind. And we may *mean* things that have never been meant before. Our capacity to produce novel utterances is one of the things that make us creative. Thus in a real sense, moment to moment, people are unique. This is how our mechanical creativity captures what is precious to the humanist.

This perspective on man may solve problems for the humanist/scientist but it creates problems for the psychologist. How do we handle incoming sentences when we are able to prove that they are creative and do not obey a strict order? This question will occupy a good deal of our attention. In what follows we shall address how linguistic theory represents creativity, and how we might build the capacity to recognize newly created sentences into a parser.

5. *Assigning Grammatical Structures to Sentences*

Sentences as Abstractions

One of the insights that Chomsky had was that a normal sentence has no definition. A normal sentence cannot be defined for the reasons we have been discussing: it could go on forever, and you would never know how much it could contain. It could be a single word like *Go!* or one of the seemingly interminable sentences that one is liable to read in a law book.

Chomsky then had the insight that the notion *sentence* did represent part of our conceptual structure if one defined it abstractly: a sentence is made up of a subject and a verb. A consequence of this move was that an ordinary sentence could actually contain many sentences. Thus, a sentence like

I think that John will ask Bill to come

actually has three sentences within it: *I think*, *John will ask Bill*, and *Bill to come*. In fact, one sentence can be contained entirely inside of another:

The boy I like sings.

Here we have *The boy sings* and *I like (the boy)*. However, we may not have a sentence in which a subject or a verb is missing:

*the boy John said.

76

This sentence is inadequate because there is no verb associated with *the boy* (as in *The boy John likes sings*). Chomsky's abstraction therefore captures an observable difference. We can tell the difference between acceptable sentences and nonsentences.

This knowledge appears to be possessed by every human being, but it also appears to be untaught. A child, simply by being exposed to language, will learn to communicate in sentences that obey this abstraction.

One might object that one of the sentences we mentioned above fails our test:

Go!

There is no subject noun here. However, there is an implicit *you* as the subject of such imperative sentences. This is evident from the fact that we can say *Wash yourself!* but not **Wash himself!* **Reflexive pronouns**, i.e., the pronouns that end in *-self* (*myself, yourself, herself* etc.), occur when the same person is referred to more than once in the same sentence. Thus, the real representation for the sentence would be (*you*) *wash yourself*, which fulfils both the requirement that a sentence have a subject and the requirement that a reflexive pronoun be linked to another noun in the same sentence.

A sentence like

John wanted to go

also appears to fail the test. The verb *go* does not have a subject noun next to it. But, if we ask ourselves who goes, or will go, in this sentence, we know that it must be *John*. This would not be the case for

John wanted Bill to go.

We are led to the conclusion that there must be an invisible second instance of *John* in the earlier sentence. Reflexive pronouns can be used here, too, to diagnose the presence of an invisible subject:

John wanted to wash himself

but

John wanted Mary to wash him.
*John wanted Mary to wash himself.

If *John* is the subject of *wash* then *himself* appears in the object position in the second sentence. However, if *Mary* is the subject of *wash* then the pronoun must be *him*. *Himself* may not appear. The abstract notion of sentence gains support from examples like these. Even when the noun is invisible we can tell when we have a sentence.

This abstraction reappears constantly. If we say

The sky thundered, and then it happened again

the *it* refers to the sentence *The sky thundered. It* does not refer to *thundered and* or just to *the sky*. Here one might object: there is nothing abstract about noun and verb. They are clearly spoken (or written), and, therefore, sentences must be perfectly concrete phenomena. It is true that most nouns and verbs are expressed, but that is not the point. The notion is that noun and verb forms a unit, but something like noun and adverb (*house quickly*) does not. The label that says 'This is a sentence' is abstract. It is present as a boundary around noun-verb pairs but is never spoken.

Many other 'formal' features in language are explicitly marked. Thus, the suffix *-tion* says, 'This is a noun', or *-ness* says, 'This is an adjective that will function as a noun': *substitute/substitution*, *eager/eagerness*. The notion *question* is marked by intonation (*You are going?*), a wh-word

78

(*Who's going?*), and/or subject-verb inversion (*Are you going?*). Why should just the notion of what we can call 'an elementary sentence' remain unmarked? The answer may be that we do not need to mark that concept if all people are able to recognize elementary sentences automatically. What is shared can be assumed. It may be that the notion of elementary sentence is a **linguistic universal.**

The term 'universal' is a mild overstatement. We ought to say, instead, *planetary* linguistic knowledge. What we mean is this: members of the species homo sapiens, as evolved on this planet, perhaps share the notion elementary sentence as a part of their biological endowment. It can be found in any language. It is arguably a mental organ like a nose or mouth or ear. We do not know if species elsewhere in the universe will look like us, though it is not impossible. The biological principles that guarantee high degrees of symmetry (two arms, two legs etc.) may be in fact universal. Efforts to equip interplanetary rockets with decipherable messages have sought to isolate which features of language are genuinely universal and which are earth-bound. However, the answers to these questions lie far beyond anything we can research systematically.

Another place in which we can find sentences is, surprisingly enough, as part of nouns. This may sound absurd at first, but if we look at phrases like the following we see that it is true:

the man who shouted

The phrase fails to be a sentence, but the **relative clause** *who shouted* in fact satisfies our definition of a sentence: it has something that serves as a noun (*who*) and something that serves as a verb (*shouted*). The phrase could be augmented to read

The man who shouted collapsed.

Now, *the man* also has a verb, *collapsed*; and we have one sentence inside another. The inner sentence, *who shouted*, has a special role – it modifies *the man*. In this sense it is an elementary sentence inside a noun, or, as we customarily refer to it, a **noun phrase**.

We can now amend our definition of a sentence to say that it consists not just of a noun and a verb, but instead, of a noun phrase and a verb. However, even this is not quite enough. We need to note that verbs do not always occur alone, as in *John sleeps*, *Bill swims*. Sometimes they are followed by an object, as in *John loves Mary*. We therefore need to say that the verb can, optionally, have an object. The word *optional* has repeatedly crept into our vocabulary. It is, therefore, part of our mental machinery and we need a way to represent it. Let us say that parentheses (round brackets) denote optional elements. Now we can summarize what we have so far:

1. A sentence = noun phrase – verb – (noun phrase)

    (I.e., a sentence is composed of a noun phrase followed by a verb followed by an optional noun phrase.)

2. A noun phrase = noun – (sentence)

    (I.e., a noun phrase is composed of a noun followed optionally by a sentence.)

We are in fact only scratching the surface here. There are other possibilities such as prepositional phrases which can come after both nouns and verbs, as in *the man in the room*, *go in the room*. But the simple definitions we have given are sufficient for the time being.

A creative mechanism. Now let us return to our task of building a mechanism that is creative. One simple device we can use to express this creativity is a 'loop', in which we make use of a set of substitutable definitions. Here are the two rules we have already discussed.

1. A sentence = noun phrase – verb – (noun phrase)
2. A noun phrase = noun – (sentence)

These two rules can be written in a kind of shorthand:

1. S $\longrightarrow$ NP V (NP)
2. NP $\longrightarrow$ N (S)

These two rules alone can be used to generate an infinite sentence. Here's how: we take a sentence, this sentence has a noun phrase (NP) in it which can have a sentence inside it, that sentence has a noun phrase in it which can have a sentence inside it, etc. Thus, we can produce sentences like this one

I saw a man who liked a boy who had a sandwich that looked like a hamburger that . . .

Words and Ideas

Now we have a mechanical kind of creativity. It is not the only dimension of creativity. There is the all-important dimension of choosing words to go into those potentially infinite loops. We have a creative process of word selection which is a function of another creative process – choosing words to match ideas. It is often thought that we think in terms of words, but a moment's reflection reveals that the notion is either blatantly wrong or fundamentally oversimplified. The very fact that we can say something and then conclude that it failed to say what we 'meant' implies that there is some sort of representation of what we mean that is outside the realm of the words that we choose to express it. In addition, there are many kinds of thought – like choosing colours when painting or analysing the offence when playing football – in which words couldn't be further from our minds. These other kinds of creativity are ones on which we have not yet got a scientific grip. We know that they are there, but no one has been able to suggest what kind of mechanism might handle them. We know, however, that the mechanism must operate very quickly. Every time we want to say something, we certainly do not search through our large vocabulary list in our heads. Something takes us quickly to just the spot we want. It is not like looking for a town on a map – which can be extremely slow even though we can scan large parts of the map at once.

We must pay close attention to word-retrieval and the 'ideas' expressed when we look at how sentences are comprehended in real-time; the 'ideas' can often be shown to play a critical role. We shall return to this topic later on. The investigation of the problem of 'lexical access' is in a largely pre-theoretical state. Many intriguing facts have been discovered through experiments, but scientists have had difficulties in integrating these facts into a coherent theory.

It is, by the way, difficulty and not importance that often dictates what scientists choose to study. No one will disagree that it would be much more interesting to know how we connect ideas to words than to know how we parse sentences. It is simply that the former has so far resisted rigorous analysis, while the latter problem appears to be somewhat more approachable, with the help of the structures and theoretical constructs provided by linguistic theory.

Transformations

When we build a successful explicit mechanism, we allow

ourselves to gain further insights into the facts. (The word 'explicit' here means 'fully specified' or 'leaving nothing to the imagination'; in other words, we are building a step-by-step, mechanical model.) Let us now take a further step by looking at how we form questions. Take the sentence

> What can I do?

The intuitive role of *what* is as the object of the verb *do*: *I can do what*, which is parallel to *I can do something*. Suppose we now want to relate these two sentences. We proposed a mechanism for this above. Following Chomsky's proposals, we suggested that we have a movement rule called a *transformation* that moves the noun phrase (NP) from the object position in a sentence to the front of the sentence. As we mentioned above, English has sentences of the kind: *NP – Verb – NP*. The transformation will say something like '*NP – Verb – wh-NP* is transformed into *wh-NP – NP – Verb – (trace)*'. Thus, something like

> You can see which star

would be transformed into

> Which star you can see (trace)?

which is not quite grammatical. We need another transformation to invert *you can* to *can you*:

> Which star can you see?

The Reality of Transformations

Now, one might ask: What is the evidence that we *really*

83

have these transformations in our heads? Oddly enough, this may not be an appropriate question to ask, but it is perhaps the most frequently asked question in the field of linguistics or psycholinguistics. Why is it not an appropriate question? The answer is that the concept of a transformation is fundamentally an abstract one, though based on tangible facts. In more pompous terms, we can say that it is an abstraction over a domain of fact. Let us explain. We, as speakers and hearers, know that the sentence *Which star can you see?* shares properties with *You can see a star*. It shares not only particular words but also the fact that we understand *star* as the object of *see* in both sentences even though in one case it is removed from its normal position after the verb. A transformation describes this factually based relation. The factual basis is our knowledge – or what is called our 'intuitions about grammaticality'. Unless the linguistic theory itself is wrong, there must be some psychological analogue to the notion of transformation.

However we choose to represent the psychological – and, ultimately, the neurological – mechanisms that determine the way in which we know that the wh-word is the object of the verb, the notion of transformation can be regarded as in some way equal to this formulation. Similarly, one might say that we either use the brakes or the gears to *brake* the forward motion of a car. What the verb *brake* refers to here is then either the gears or the brake. The actual psychological or neurological realization of a transformation might be a pure reflection of the notion of transformation (like the brakes), or it may be a more complex interactive mechanism that accomplishes the same thing (like the gears). In this sense the original question is not the right one to ask. We should ask instead how the concept of transformation is realized or made concrete in terms of real-time processing. We do not need to ask whether the psychological evidence proves it right or wrong.

84

Assigning Grammatical Structures to Sentences

There have been a number of experiments that address this question. The focus has been on the problem of what one does with information about sentence structure as it arrives. Suppose we begin a sentence with *What did you* .... What have we got so far? We know that a question has been started, but we do not know what is being asked. There are various possibilities:

What did you think —— ran away?
What did you think Bill liked ——?
What did you buy ——?
What did you sit on ——?
What did you buy ——, and Mary sell ——?
What did you think that John believed Fred had tried to get Mary to do ——?

The ambiguities do not end here. We find in fact that in this kind of sentence the first wh-word can be ambiguous between subject and object:

Who is John?
Who is John going to see ——?
Who is John going to ask —— to go to town?

In the sentence *Who is John?* the *who* belongs right where it is in the subject position of the sentence. In *Who is John going to ask to go to town?* the *who* must eventually function as the subject of *to go*. So we cannot decide right away that the *who* is where it belongs if we hear *Who is John* ... Somehow all of this processing is so easy for us that we are unaware that we may be holding the *who* in our minds without a definite function until we find out where it belongs. One experiment, which we shall turn to shortly, suggests that holding on to the *who* does require extra mental effort, although this extra effort is not something that we can 'feel'.

Let us reflect for a moment on the kind of process we are

talking about. The capacity to move an element of a sentence to a new position that is indefinitely far from its origin may be a special characteristic of human beings. We do it effortlessly, because we are 'designed' to do it; and it is special to, or characteristic of, human beings in the same way that the motion of a gazelle, again, effortless, can only be accomplished by a gazelle. This is, at least, the hypothesis. The reader can ask himself as we examine the details of English whether he thinks that the kind of knowledge we have and use every day could really be learned or if understanding language is like opening one's eyes and seeing. For language we must open our ears, make connections between words and things, and adjust our grammars in some slight ways. The rest may be all there. Making 'slight adjustments' and a few 'connections between words and things' can be taken to refer to the special characteristics of each language. Such operations seem monumental to those in language classes or to tourists trying to make themselves understood in a foreign country, but they may actually be quite minimal. It is like noticing that human beings all look quite different from each other; but, in many respects, we all look exactly the same.

An Experiment about *Who* and Time

Eric Wanner and Michael Maratsos (1978) devised an experiment to show that we do extra work when we must hold on to a wh-word without assigning it a function. What they did was to contrast sentences like these two:

The witch who despised sorcerers frightened little children.
The witch who sorcerers despised —— frightened little children.

In the first sentence there is virtually no point at which the function of *who* is unclear. When the verb *despised* arrives, we know that *who* must be its subject. In the second sentence, there is an unresolved unclarity until we realize that *who* is the object of *despised.* Wanner and Maratsos had constructed a model of a sentence processor in which they proposed a special bit of memory which they called the HOLD spot. This was where incomplete information was held until it could be incorporated into the analysis of a sentence. Later, when the information was integrated into the sentential analysis, it would be shipped off to some sort of long-term memory. In this long-term memory, it is presumed that we store information about the meaning of the sentence, but little information about its actual grammatical form. If we were to ask ourselves tomorrow what the test sentences were about, we would probably remember that they had something to do with witches, sorcerers and scaring children, and little more. That is, we would remember the gist of the sentences but not their actual syntactic forms. The HOLD mechanism, however, is postulated to be a special-purpose memory that operates during syntactic parsing.

Wanner and Maratsos guessed that using the HOLD mechanism would absorb some of the mental effort that might be used for other purposes; so they decided to perform an experiment in which they gave subjects an additional task to do during the time they were trying to understand sentences. The prediction was that in the first sentence, where the HOLD mechanism really doesn't come into play, subjects would not need to expend any extra effort in processing the sentence. However, in the second sentence, where *who* must be held on HOLD for a little while, subjects would need to expend some extra effort, and this would make them unable to perform the additional task as well as they had done with sentences like the first one.

Here is what they did. They presented a sentence, word

by word, to their subjects. Somewhere along the line, the sentence would be interrupted by a list of five proper names. Subjects had to remember the sentence because they were tested on their comprehension after the sentence was presented, and they also had to remember as many of the names in the list as they could. In the first sentence (above), the list of names appeared just after the subject had read *The witch who despised*; in the second sentence, the list appeared after *The witch who sorcerers*. After the list of names appeared, the rest of the sentence was presented. The idea here is that subjects who were interrupted in the second sentence would have a harder time remembering the list of names because of the additional effort they had to devote to holding on to the *who*, which could not be assigned a grammatical function at that point. Readers may themselves be able to feel the difference in difficulty between these two sentence fragments. In both cases, the subject must remember the sentence fragment as a whole because it has not been completed. The test sentences were interspersed with a number of control sentences in which the interruptions occurred in places other than the middle of the sentence so that subjects could not predict exactly where they would be interrupted by the list.

Wanner and Maratsos found a sharp statistical difference between the subjects' performance on the two types of sentences. As predicted, they found that subjects had a harder time remembering the names in the list in sentences like the second. (That is, the subjects were able to remember fewer names on the list in these cases.) This gives us indirect evidence that an energy-consuming operation was being carried out that correlates with the application of the transformation of wh-movement. Since we regard the operation of a transformation as abstract – or at least interior – we cannot expect to find a direct method for showing its presence. Anything that is not overtly observable can only be demonstrated through indirect means. All we are saying is that the sentence which, according to a transformational grammar, had had a wh-word moved out of its 'normal' place in the sentence was also the one which subjects had difficulty in comprehending. It is as if they were holding the wh-word in their minds until they found a place where it might fit.

Method and theory. Psychologists make a substantial attempt to be 'hard-headed' in drawing their conclusions and, therefore, seek to demonstrate that extraneous factors are not the source of their results. If one examines the sentences used by Wanner and Maratsos, one finds that there is a word order difference between the two kinds of sentences. If there is an experimental effect but two potential sources of difference in the test materials, then one must show that one difference (the one that interests us) is the one that produces the difference in performance. Therefore one needs to show that the transformational difference, which fits the theory of the HOLD mechanism, caused the increased memory load and not the word order difference. This reasoning is 'logical' but it is not altogether scientific. The reason that it is not scientific is that there is no existing theory which one could use to argue plausibly that the word order difference is the source of the problem. There is, however, a large and complex linguistic theory that justifies the interpretation of the effect in terms of a transformation. Therefore, if no other experiments were possible and if no plausible alternative theory came to light, the results could be taken to support the claim that a transformation of wh-movement corresponds to some real-time mental computation.

In any case, further experiments were done which effectively eliminated the difference in word order as a possible cause of the difference in subjects' performance on the two kinds of sentences.

Transformations and Complexity

We have seen that wh-movement can operate in a wide variety of fairly subtle syntactic contexts. We have, however, barely scraped the surface. A set of fairly simple rules will generate a large number of complex forms. It is 'simple' if you know what the rules are, but amazingly complex if you do not. What kinds of complexity can be generated? First, let us observe that wh-movement is not the only movement rule. There is also a rule that moves ordinary nouns, or, more accurately, noun phrases (NPs). NP-movement occurs in sentences like these:

> John was hit ——.
> John is easy to see ——.

In both of these sentences we find that *John* is understood as the object of the verb (*hit* or *see*). Therefore we may propose that a transformation exists which moves a noun phrase from object to subject position.

> [empty NP position] was hit John ——→
> John was hit (trace)

The moved NP can also come from far away in the sentence:

> John was believed to have been chosen to be seen —— by the Queen.

So far we have reproduced the same kinds of evidence that we used to argue for the rule of wh-movement. We can use the two rules together to create additional complexity, combining the two operations in the same sentence to produce two 'gaps'.

> A piano is easy to play sonatas on ——.

90

A sonata is easy to play —— on a piano.
What is a sonata easy to play —— on ——?

We have now moved both an NP and a wh-word, and we now have two gaps in the sentence. Once again, our system of mental computation remains unfazed. However, the system can be easily upset if we perform the two movement operations in reverse order.

Unintelligible:
What is a piano easy to play —— on ——?

Now, we know from the sentences above that both the object of *play* (*sonata(s)*) and the object of the preposition *on* (*piano*) can be moved to the subject position. In addition, they can both be moved to the wh-position at the front, as in

What is it easy to play —— on a violin?
What is it easy to play a sonata on ——?

If we do both wh-movement and NP-movement at once, however, then *What is a sonata easy to play on?* is possible, but *What is a piano easy to play on?* is ruled out. Why does this peculiar asymmetry exist? If both operations are possible, why must they be applied in one order and not the other? We do not know immediately whether the problem with the impossible sentence is that it is not English or whether it is English (i.e., allowed by the rules of English grammar) but just difficult to comprehend.

The answers to these questions are not entirely clear (Fodor, 1978, 1979). But let us explore one possibility. We will try to explain the difficulty in terms of a memory device. Notice that if we draw lines to connect the moved words with their gaps there is no crossing of lines in the first sentence (as shown below), but there is in the second:

91

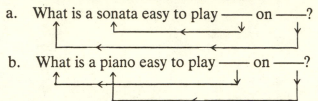

a.   What is a sonata easy to play —— on ——?

b.   What is a piano easy to play —— on ——?

Notice now that the word *piano* could, in the second sentence, be the object of the verb *play* as well as the object of the preposition *on*. Now let us do a little thought experiment. If we have the incomplete sentence *What is a piano easy to play*, how might we imagine that it will finish? We might try to imagine something of the form: *What is a piano easy to play —— in comparison to ——?* (E.g., *It is easy to play the piano in comparison to the organ.*) Here we are forcing the word *piano* into the first available hole or gap in the sentence. In other words, we are trying to make a sentence like (b) into one like (a) in which the lines connecting the moved words to their gaps do not cross. One way to imagine this relationship is in terms of what is called a **push-down stack**. Suppose that our little bit of working memory, the HOLD mechanism, is like a stack of dishes in which we put new items to remember on top of one another. The last thing we put on the stack will be the first one we take off. (I.e., there is no pulling things out of the middle of the stack or from the bottom allowed.) If we put things on the stack in the order 1, 2, 3, then we will have to take them out in the order 3, 2, 1. If we depict this relationship linearly and draw lines between the numbers that match, we find that the lines do not cross, creating a pattern like the one in sentence (a), above.

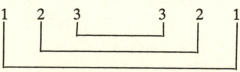

Suppose, then, that we let the grammar generate forms like (b), above. The working memory system, because of its structure, will not be able to handle them, however; and they will be ruled out as unacceptable, i.e., incomprehensible. The structure of the working memory is such that the order in which things can be taken out of memory is the reverse of the order in which they are put in, thus creating structures that are 'nested' inside one another. This suggestion should be viewed as nothing more than a hypothesis at this point. However, it is an ideal illustration of how the structure of two systems – an abstract grammar and a real-time sentence processor – could interact to predict fairly subtle differences between acceptability and grammaticality.

Some Support for the Hypothesis

Now we shall do what scientists often do: we shall see just how far we can push our generalization that fillers and gaps must be 'nested' and not cut across one another. Let us try a long sentence (following Fodor, 1979):

> *Which children*$_1$ did Carol say *this book*$_2$ was too difficult to read ——$_2$ to ——$_1$?

(Note that we have had to resort to using subscripts to indicate which NP goes with which gap in this sentence.) Here, as predicted, we find that the mirror-image, nested structure (1, 2, 2, 1) works. On the other hand, when nesting is not maintained, the sentence becomes virtually impossible to understand. Note first that we can say things like

> I read the children the book.

That is, an indirect object can occur immediately after a verb and before the direct object. Now notice that the following variant of our long sentence fails:

Which children$_1$ did Carol say *this book*$_2$ was too difficult to read ———$_1$ ———$_2$?

Here the dependencies between the fillers and gaps are intersecting, and not nested inside one another. Of course, in this case one might guess that the problem lies not in the lack of the nesting relationship but in the fact that the two gaps occur next to one another at the end of the sentence. We can discount this suggestion, though. The following sentence shows that gaps can be adjacent if they preserve nesting:

At which distance$_1$ is *the chart*$_2$ easiest for you to read ———$_2$ ———$_1$?

This works because we assume that the original sentence was something like

It is easiest for you to read the chart at which distance.

Where do we go from here? We might next ask what happens if, instead of moving phrases to the front of sentences, we move them to the end; that is, if we move them to the right instead of to the left. Rightward movement occurs quite frequently in English sentences. Note the relations between these pairs of sentences:

I gave a beautifully illustrated book about butterflies to Fred.
I gave ———$_1$ to Fred *a beautifully illustrated book about butterflies*$_1$.
I need a lamp that is very bright on my desk.
I need a lamp ———$_1$ on my desk *that is very bright*$_1$.

The existence of such rightward movements means that the parsing system cannot always assume that a moved constituent comes first and a gap later. The gap may precede the moved constituent. The processor must therefore have some flexibility. In effect, it must recognize and store gaps as well as moved words or phrases. We shall see shortly what happens if our so-called HOLD mechanism must store both gaps and words at once. But let us now return to rightward movement. Must rightward movement also obey our nesting constraint? The sentences below indicate that it must.

a. (Original sentence)
No one who wants to be a friend of mine puts things that would block it into the sink.
b. (Nested version)
No one ———$_1$ puts things ———$_2$ into the sink *that would block it$_2$ who wants to be a friend of mine$_1$.*
c. (Unprocessible with intersecting dependencies)
No one ———$_1$ puts things ———$_2$ into the sink *who wants to be a friend of mine$_1$ that would block it$_2$.*

In (c) it is only when we hear the final phrase *that would block it* that the sentence becomes unprocessible, or at least very difficult to process. Without this phrase we would have a single gap in the sentence and no intersection would occur:

No one puts things into the sink who wants to be a friend of mine.

Now our generalization begins to look robust. We have seen that it works for both leftward and rightward movement.

Extending the Hypothesis

So far so good. But the postulated HOLD mechanism requires some elaboration. We cannot automatically assume that every nested example can be interpreted as easily as those above. Consider the following:

a. *What*$_1$ did *John*$_2$ intend ——$_2$ to do ——$_1$?
b. **What*$_1$ did *who*$_2$ intend ——$_2$ to do ——$_1$?

The reader should note that the (b) sentence should be read with *normal* intonation, i.e., with the same intonation as the (a) sentence. There is an acceptable version of (b) in which the *who* receives extra heavy stress: *What did WHO intend to do?* This form is what is known as an **echo question,** and it is usually used in cases where the hearer didn't catch all of the speaker's sentence, as in an interchange like the one below:

> *Speaker:* What did (mumble) intend to do?
> *Hearer:* What did WHO intend to do?

Now, when the (b) sentence is read with normal intonation it is distinctly odd; yet it has the same structure as the (a) sentence except that it has *who* where (a) has *John.* What is happening here? It seems that double-gap sentences are possible as long as only one of the gaps is to be filled by a wh-word. The next sentence shows that a sentence may contain two wh-words, but only if one of them is left in its original place:

> *Who*$_1$ did John want ——$_1$ to do *what*?

Thus far we have discussed mainly how the HOLD mechanism deals with wh-words. Let us now look at some examples of how it copes with ordinary nouns. We noted earlier that there was a gap in sentences like

> John is easy to see ——

where *John* is interpreted as the object of *see.* Note that the

96

beginning of this sentence gives no indication that there is a gap to follow. This seems to suggest that HOLD must store all nouns for possible reference to upcoming gaps. But it would be incorrect to say that HOLD stores only single nouns. Suppose we have a sentence of the form:

Sidney, Norman and Fred were easy to see ———.

It would be incorrect to say that Fred was the only one who was easy to see, just because *Fred* is the closest noun to the verb *see*. All three nouns are obviously meant to fill the gap. It is impossible to say something like

*Sidney, Norman and Fred were easy to see two of ———.

The expression *Sidney, Norman and Fred* is a unit, one noun phrase that is composed of three separate noun phrases. Obviously, then, noun phrases can have complex inner structure.

The HOLD mechanism will also have to be sensitive to sentences within noun phrases:

The cat that I like is easy to see ———.

If HOLD contained only the phrase *the cat* it would be unfaithful to the meaning of this sentence. The full information *the cat that I like* is necessary when the gap is filled. In order to make the HOLD mechanism work, we have to refer to the concept *noun phrase*, although this is an abstract concept that involves 'invisible' boundaries. Thus we find that the ability to use language entails utilization of a general cognitive ability. But the general cognitive ability must make reference to abstract definitions given by the grammar of the language.

A Substantial Challenge

In a way, what we have observed about gap-filling and mirror-image nested structures may seem obvious. However, we have been ignoring an important body of evidence that appears to straightforwardly contradict our claims that intersecting dependencies between gaps and fillers do not exist (following Solan, 1980).

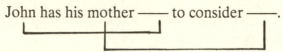

John has his mother —— to consider ——.

This sentence appears to have exactly the kind of intersecting system of dependencies that we have tried to rule out. The sentence above means 'John must consider his mother' and not 'John's mother must consider him'. At first glance, this evidence might lead us to abandon our model.

It is at moments like this that some important insights are necessary. When Newton claimed that gravity existed and that it affected all objects in the same way, he had to overlook some very powerful counterevidence. Birds fly, steam rises, and leaves and feathers fall slowly to the ground. All these things seem to contradict, at least superficially, the claim that the force of gravity affects all objects in the same way. Newton required two concepts at once: the notion of a constant gravitational force and a variable factor, friction or air-resistance. It is air-resistance (the force of friction produced by movement through air) that interacts with the surface of leaves and feathers and with the wings of birds and which obscures the role of gravity in each case.

We are potentially in the same situation here. If we can claim that there is some other intervening variable at work here, then we might be able to explain how our model works in some contexts and fails in others. We have already noted that some intersecting dependencies are possible (*John has his mother to consider*) and others are impossible

(*No one puts things in the sink who wants to be a friend of mine that would block it*). Has our reasoning up to this point been faulty?

Let us first note that just about all of the examples of filler-gap dependencies that we have considered up to this point have not involved subjects of infinitives. Typically, our examples have involved the objects of verbs and prepositions. That is, we have been dealing with sentences like:

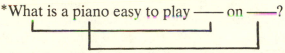

Let us now take a closer look at some simple sentences in which infinitives without subjects occur:

John expected —— to leave.

It is clear that John, and not someone else, is the person who expects to leave. Remember that we have defined sentences as things that have a subject and a verb. Verbs must have subjects; therefore, *leave* must have one, and it appears to be *John* in this sentence. In linguistic terminology, the noun phrase *John* **controls** the subject position of *leave*. Let us also note that the subject of an infinitive, in many cases, does not need to be someone specific – or even someone mentioned in the same sentence. Hamlet was trying to claim that everyone was involved in a similar dilemma when he said *To be, or not to be*. But the subject of the verb is not an implicit 'everyone' in a sentence like *John expected to leave*.

The relation between *John* and *leave* in our sentence involves another kind of important relation in grammars: **coreference**, which means, literally, 'referring to the same person or thing'. If we said:

John decided he should leave

we would find that *he* is John, at least in one reading of the sentence. In other words, *John* and *he* are coreferential. In a way, this coreferential relation is much like the relation between *John* and the gap in *John expected —— to leave.*

It would be incorrect to claim that movement was involved in such cases:

*—— expected John to leave.

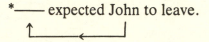

John has not moved from the subject position of *to leave.* The noun phrase *John* simply has two functions: that of expecter and leaver. Therefore, we need a mechanism different from the movement one to capture the relationship.

One of the ways that have been proposed by linguists to capture this relationship is a deletion transformation. It is proposed that in the deep structures for such sentences there are two NPs, one for each of the subject positions. The origin of *John expected to leave* would be a sentence like

John expected John to leave.

The second instance of *John* is deleted because it is identical to the subject NP of the main sentence. In linguistic terminology, we say that the second NP is **deleted under identity** with the first NP. If the two NPs are not identical, then the second NP will not be deleted, as in

John expected Bill to leave.

The second instance of the NP will never appear on the surface in the language. This is an interesting fact. If it is correct, it means that the mind has a model that it uses to derive sentences that are spoken and heard which is never itself spoken or heard. Thus, the relation between *John* and the gap in *John expected to leave* is different from that between the gap filler and the gap in most of the sentences we have considered up to now. For a hearer to comprehend *John expected to leave*, he must construct – or reconstruct – an 'origin' sentence that is entirely mental.

We are now beginning to refine our mechanism: we cannot discuss merely the relation between fillers and gaps because there are two kinds of relations – a **movement relation** and a **deletion relation**. The constraint against intersecting dependencies appears to work only when there are two movements involved and not when there is a deletion involved. We can think of solid lines as indicating movement relations, and deletion relations as being indicated by dotted lines:

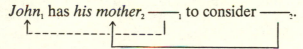

In order for our constraint against intersecting dependencies to apply, the lines that intersect will have to be of the same type.

The cautious reader might now object: we have simply used a bit of sneaky sleight-of-hand here to escape from the fact that our constraint does not work. The fact remains, though, that if we assume that there is some sort of HOLD mechanism with the structure we have postulated (a push-down stack), then the mechanism can only 'see' the NP that is on the top of the 'stack'. It has no access to NPs that are further down on the stack. This structure will block any attempt to relate a gap to a noun that is not on the top of the stack. This is the kind of situation one gets into when one commits oneself to building a mechanistic model. We cannot escape our problem by remodelling the HOLD mechanism in any obvious way. We must somehow argue that subject-identity must be dealt with by a different mechanism. We are now in a position in which we must argue that there are two mechanisms which interact in what seem like confusing ways. We shall continue now to talk about more facts that our new mechanism must deal with.

But first, let us recapitulate: we have observed that there is some sort of mirror-image limitation on certain sentences in English. We can account for this limitation with a postulated HOLD mechanism that works with a push-down stack. However, we have other sentences, those which involve filling infinitive subject gaps, which simply will not fit into that model.

A Possible Solution

Let us assume that information about empty subjects of infinitives is part of the grammar (i.e., it is part of one's knowledge of the language), but that the use of this information does not involve the use of the little bit of memory in our HOLD mechanism. That is, a hearer does not make any decisions about how to fill empty subject positions in infinitives until he has recognized that there is a subject gap. When the hearer encounters an infinitive subject gap, he will 'know' that it is the same as the subject of the main clause.

John decided yesterday morning, just before lunch,
—— to go.

The hearer who finds the gap simply *knows* that the subject of the infinitive is identical to the subject of the main clause. He must remember what that subject is, but he has not previously put that information on the stack.

We should, then, expect to find no memory effects in such situations. We would not expect to find the same effects — or lack of effects — with wh-words because we know that there will be a gap as soon as we hear them and we know that we must find out what their functions are in the sentence. We know that the wh-word must have some role in the sentence, but until we know where it fits we cannot know what that role is. Therefore, we must hold it in memory until we know where it goes. We thus have made the hypothesis that there is a HOLD mechanism that is part of the language processor and functions as a sort of auxiliary device to the grammar. (Note: there is an intuitive sense in which the HOLD mechanism must be correct – insofar as it appears to be the best way to capture the facts that we have been discussing. There are problems with it, however, which we will discuss later. In particular, the way in which moved NPs that are not wh-noun phrases are connected to gaps is not easily taken care of. There are some proposals (Bresnan, 1983) that therefore try to treat *all* instances of NP movement as deletion rather than movement.)

We have proposed that some decisions involved in understanding sentences involve the HOLD mechanism and that other, apparently similar, decisions do not. However, the interpretation of subjectless infinitives certainly takes place 'on-line'. Therefore, some form of memory must be involved. When a hearer gets to the gap, he must not have forgotten the beginning of the sentence. One way to think about the difference between subjects of infinitives and wh-words is this. To capture the subject of an infinitive we simply go *back* and refer to what we already know: the subject of the main clause. For wh-words, the memory problem goes *forward*: we must hold on to information for later use because we are unsure just where this information will be needed.

In effect, we must have two kinds of memory. The first kind is memory that we know we must have and use all the time in understanding sentences: we have to remember what the grammatical roles of various noun phrases are in a sentence if we are to get the message conveyed by the sentence. The second kind of memory is a sort of 'special-purpose' memory that comes into play only when we must remember the order in which moved constituents have occurred in a sentence. We should expect to see the effects of the second kind of memory, then, in experiments like the one by Wanner and Maratsos (discussed above, page 86) because *extra* memory is needed to handle moved constituents. In cases in which we must remember only those things which we must remember anyway, we should expect to see no effects.

Another Problem

Another problem!?! The reader may think that we have made life complex enough with our various examples. But the complexity we illustrate comes not from a desire to be perplexing but from a desire to give the reader a fuller sense of just what his language faculty can accomplish.

We have articulated two systems of rules: a system of movement rules that requires a HOLD mechanism, and a system of noun-identity rules that straightforwardly makes use of mechanisms that we have argued must exist in order to understand *any* sentence. Now we will complicate matters a little bit by showing that these two systems can operate together. It is possible to *move* a wh-word from the subject position of an infinitive.

Who do you want to visit?

This is an ambiguous sentence. It can mean something like 'Who do you want to visit you?' or 'Who do you, personally, intend to visit?' In other words, the *who* could have come from either the subject position of the infinitive or the object position of the infinitive. Therefore, we must amend our statement that a person confronted with a subjectless infinitive simply takes the subject of the main clause to be the subject. If a wh-word is involved, the hearer must consider the possibility that there is a *movement* gap in the infinitive subject position. Since the same gap could have been produced by two different operations, we are forced to state a relationship between them. The relationship, as we have seen, cannot be one that prohibits intersecting dependencies since we know that they may occur in cases like these.

How does the hearer deal with overlapping possibilities? There is a fundamental key: the verb. Verbs carry information not only about their meanings but also about the kinds of syntax that they allow in their environments. Thus, the verb *want* can take either a subjectless infinitive or one with a subject:

> I want to visit Rodney.
> I want Rodney to visit.

Other verbs like *try* and *decide* allow only subjectless infinitives:

> Malcolm decided to go.
> *Malcolm decided Carl to go.
> *Who did Malcolm decide to go?
> Doug tried to go.
> *Doug tried Mike to go.
> *Who did Doug try to go?

If a verb requires that the main clause subject and the subject of an infinitive complement be identical, then it follows that a wh-word cannot be used to provide a different subject for the infinitive. Other verbs require that the *object* of the main clause be the subject of the infinitive:

> John told Mary to go.
> *John told to go.
> Who did John tell to go?

Understanding and Producing Speech

A verb like *tell*, therefore, has different characteristics: it must have a subject for the infinitive that is different from the subject of the main clause, and we can have a question in which we 'extract' a *who* from the subject position of the infinitive phrase.

Problems arise when the verb is ambiguous. Then, one must wait until the subordinate clause arrives before one knows how to analyse the main clause verb. Consider the following examples of one-clause sentences:

     a. Who did you walk to the store?
     b. Who did you walk to the store with?

The verb *walk* is ambiguous between a transitive reading (*I walked Bill home*) and an intransitive reading (*I walked home*). The intransitive reading can occur with a prepositional phrase: *I walked home with Bill*. As we hear the sentences (a) and (b), above, we do not know when we get to the verb *walk* whether it will be transitive or intransitive. That is, we do not know if we should stick in *who* after the verb or wait to see if later on in the sentence there is a preposition that needs an object. If in sentence (b) we stick in *who* too early we will get: *You walked who to the store with ——?* We will then have to go back, take out the *who*, and put it in after the preposition in order to get the right result: *You walked to the store with who?* If we do not stick in *who* after *walk* but continue to the end of the sentence, we may discover that our sentence is (a) and that we have ended up with *You walked to the store (who)*. (We have left the *who* in parentheses because we really wouldn't know what to do with it at this stage.) We then must go back and stick the *who* in after the verb. One can often 'feel' these processes of 'reanalysis'. If one can feel this 'reanalysis' then our experience of mental complexity corresponds to what our theory says should be complex. If something feels simple in our experience but looks complex in the theory, then we have a potential problem. But, if complications

106

arise both in our intuitions about complexity and in our statement of theoretical alternatives, this is a good sign for the theory. In other words, it is acceptable for a theory to look quite complex, even distressingly and unnaturally complex, if the phenomena to be explained show complex characteristics. Fortunately, we have arrived at a domain of complexity that is open to experimental investigation – to which we will turn shortly.

We have seen that verbs carry syntactic information with them. But occasionally we can receive another kind of advance information that can help us choose one possibility over another. For instance, take the sentence:

Which dog did Steve walk to the store?

We have a tendency to take the transitive reading for *walk* here because it is more common to say *Steve walked the dog* than it is to say *Steve walked with the dog*. Both are possible, however. Thus, the decision about where to put a moved wh-phrase will be a function of (1) where there is a possible gap, (2) what verb is being used, and (3) which reading, if there is more than one, is favoured by the use of particular words in the sentence.

Suppose you encountered the sentence:

Which dog did Steve walk to the store with?

And suppose that you initially made the incorrect guess that *which dog* followed *walk*. When you got to the preposition *with* there must have been a moment when you undid the first, wrong analysis and chose another. The moment can last just a few milliseconds (i.e., just about imperceptible) or longer, if the correct analysis is hard to get at. Remember how difficult it was to comprehend the sentence

The man who hunts ducks out on weekends.

107

Here the process is difficult because the context (i.e., the words used) strongly suggests that *hunts ducks* is a verb phrase, with *hunts* as a transitive verb taking *ducks* as its noun phrase object. It takes quite a bit of effort to overcome this tendency and to come up with the correct reanalysis.

We can express the distinction in processing strategies that we have been discussing here by advancing two hypotheses about how the HOLD mechanism operates: (A) unload the HOLD stack at the end of the sentence or (B) unload an NP from the HOLD stack each time a gap occurs. Thus, we have two guesses about how we use the HOLD mechanism:

(A) All moved NPs are kept in the HOLD stack, at the end of the sentence they are assigned to gaps according to the mirror-image requirement that rules out intersecting dependencies.

(B) NPs are assigned to gaps as the gaps occur; when a gap is encountered, the noun on the top of the stack is used to fill the gap. If a mistake is made, the parser must go back and reanalyse the sentence. Mistakes will occur if there are NPs left on the stack at the end of the sentence or if there are unfilled gaps in the sentence.

These two hypotheses have different implications for processing. If we follow the first strategy we would not assign fillers to gaps until we knew exactly where the gaps were. If we follow the second strategy we would put the filler on the top of the stack into the first *possible* gap that we would encounter. If we are right, then we will be able to process the sentence very rapidly because we will fill gaps immediately, and we will not have to keep a bunch of fillers and gaps in memory until the end of the sentence. If we are wrong, we will have to go back and take the NPs out of the wrong places and reanalyse. This should take time – though, perhaps, not a whole lot of time.

We now have two strategies that people might use, both of which will produce the appropriate mirror-image dependency structure. We can call one the 'wait until the end strategy' and the other the 'fill the gaps as you go along strategy'. In (A) fillers and gaps are matched up when the sentence is over; in (B) we fill gaps as we encounter them. Notice that strategy (A) is essentially a conservative strategy: it may take longer, but it is considerably less likely to lead us into error. The (B) strategy may be more efficient in many cases, but it can lead us into costly mistakes in others. Which of these is the one that people follow? We shall discuss an experiment which was designed to find an answer to this question.

The Experiment

Frazier, Clifton, and Randall (1983) conducted a carefully controlled experiment to address some of these questions. They wanted to know whether people waited until the end of a sentence to fill gaps or whether they filled gaps as they went along. They also wanted to know which fillers people would use in cases where there seemed to be more than one possibility. They looked at contrasts between sentences like these:

a. Everyone liked the woman who the little child begged —— to sing those stupid French songs for ——.

b. Everyone liked the woman who the little child started to sing those stupid French songs for ——.

Notice that in (a) the sentence is ambiguous as it is being processed: the child could either 'beg to sing' or 'beg the woman to sing'. There are two possibilities: either *the little child* is chosen automatically as the subject of *sing*, or the meaning is chosen which dictates that the woman is the singer. Either the 'automatic' subject (*the little child*) or the 'moved' subject (*the woman*) must be chosen. If the person makes the wrong decision, he should have to back up when he hears *for* at the end. The ambiguity arises because *beg* can have more than one type of construction after it. In sentence (b) there should never be this kind of ambiguity because it would not be appropriate to say 'the child started the woman to sing'.

There are many features in a well-designed psycholinguistic experiment. The sentences should be matched for length. The order in which the sentences are presented to the subjects must be controlled. The rate at which they are presented to the subjects must be controlled. And various extraneous variables that might arise because of the words used in the sentences must also be controlled. Many of these controls are difficult to carry out perfectly because, for instance, the meaning of a particular verb may vary from subject to subject. However, it is wise to minimize the effects of irrelevant factors as much as possible. Occasionally, it is necessary to use statistical methods to 'factor out' the effects of irrelevant variables after the fact when the variables cannot be systematically controlled through careful construction of the stimulus materials.

In this experiment, there were 48 sentences like the ones above. The 48 subjects who participated in the experiment were given the sentences one word at a time. The words in a sentence were presented at a rate of three words per second. In front of the subject were two buttons. The subject was instructed to push one button if he 'got it' (understood the whole sentence on the first pass) and the other if he 'missed it' (needed to go back and reread the sentence). A millisecond timer was used to measure how long it took the subject to push the button. (A millisecond is one-thousandth of a second; we abbreviate the unit as 'msec.'.)

The results are quite interesting. They show that there is some sort of measurable mental activity that is measured in msecs. And they lend support to what most psychologists believe: that we do more than simply 'recognize' or 'fail to recognize' something (like a face) and that we perform split-second computations on information that comes in through the senses.

Now, on to the results. The mean response time for comprehension of sentences like the one in (b) was 1071 msec. (just over a second); and the mean response time for sentences like the one in (a) was 1165 msec. This one-tenth-of-a-second difference between response times showed up consistently and was shown to be statistically significant. That is, it is a reliable difference. It therefore appears that it took subjects longer to restore a moved constituent to its origin than it did for them to interpret a missing infinitival subject as identical to a previous subject. This lends support to the hypothesis that gaps that arise because of movement are handled differently from those that arise because of deletion under identity. (There may, of course, be other ways of interpreting this result.)

There is also another interesting result. Further analysis of the data revealed that there was no difference in the way subjects treated ambiguous sentences as opposed to unambiguous ones, independent of the movement vs deletion contrast. This is surprising because one might imagine that a subject who hears a potentially ambiguous verb (like *beg*) would know that filling gaps as he goes along might be wrong. However, the subjects seem to do this anyway. When they get to the end of the sentence and find that they are wrong they must undo the earlier decision.

Therefore, it appears that subjects followed strategy (B) (fill the gaps as you go along) rather than strategy (A) (wait until the end), even though the more conservative strategy

111

(A) would virtually guarantee errorless performance. It seems that subjects preferred to maximize efficiency (i.e., to minimize the number of things they must hold in memory) at the expense of being led to wrong analyses on occasion.

Let us look at things in slightly more concrete terms. When the subject following strategy (B) encounters a sentence like

> Everyone likes the woman the child begged —— to sing those songs

he assumes that *the child* is the subject of *sing*. At the end of the sentence he will find that the noun phrase *the woman* has not been assigned a syntactic function. Therefore he will have to go back and remove *the child* from the subject position of *sing* and insert *the woman* in its place. If the sentence in fact had a position for *the woman*, then the analysis could proceed without a hitch:

> Everyone likes the woman the child begged —— to sing those songs for ——.

Choosing *the child* as the subject of *sing* here would be just like choosing *the child* as subject in something like *the child started to sing*. The ambiguity of *beg* has no impact on the rapidity of comprehension when the sentence actually has *the child* as subject of *sing*. If this is not the case the sentence must be reanalysed at some cost in comprehension time.

Conclusion

What, then, have we found? We have reasoned as carefully as we can using linguistic information (what is grammatical and what is not), intuitions about processing difficulty, and experimental results. We have not tried to prove that one kind of evidence is valid (e.g., intuitions) by using other kinds of evidence (e.g., experimental results). We have used all the evidence we could gather in a common quest to construct a mechanism for both describing grammatical knowledge outside of time and processing linguistic information in time. In effect, to the extent that we have succeeded, one kind of evidence does validate another. If one form of evidence were invalid, then we might expect no generalizations at all to emerge.

The fact that we have arrived at a system of definitions in which a grammar and a parser are interwoven constitutes support for both systems. There is a kind of intimately governed interaction between real-time information processing, memory, and a grammar. In the one case, we have a system of atemporal grammatical knowledge, and, in the other, a system of mechanisms for deciphering linguistic information as it comes in.

There are those who would argue differently: grammar will disappear when parsing mechanisms are fully understood. Their claim is that all of the knowledge that appears to be atemporal is in fact illusory conscious reflections upon what is a series of time-bound procedures for comprehension. They would substitute for each of our grammatical notions a notion of how sentences are understood word by word. These perspectives are hotly debated within the field although it may be fair to say that the subtlety of description and predictive power attained by current grammars has not been attained by purely procedural formulations.

We believe that the kind of system outlined in this chapter reflects the most likely answer to these questions. Grammars and parsers are modular systems designed to be intimately connected. A parser cannot be formulated or 'understood' unless it presupposes notions that come from the grammar. The deepest principles of grammar cannot be understood properly unless their relation to a parser is articulated. Each of the two systems, though intertwined, has some principles that lie outside of or work against the other system. Thus, some parsing principles may be needed just where the grammar leads us into unacceptable ambiguity; and some principles of grammar may cause the opposite result from those dictated by the parser.

Before we conclude this chapter it is perhaps wise to recall another reason for the separation of grammatical components. Our focus has been on problems of comprehension, but a human being must have the facility for production as well. There is not much known about how we construct sentences in time (although see Chapter 7). It might be the case that sentence production is very easy and sentence perception is very difficult. Consequently, the details of the linguistic system may be dictated by perception problems and not production problems, since only the former would provide any real challenge. However, the fact that most people sometimes have great difficulty in producing speech while having no difficulty in comprehending it, and the fact that virtually all people make many false starts, add *ums* and *ahs*, and often speak ungrammatically, suggests that production may be making quite a number of very substantial demands on our linguistic system.

The grammar is, then, a sort of middle-man between speech and hearing – production and perception. It has exactly the usefulness of a mental map: we can conveniently calculate a route in either direction in time – going or coming – or output and input – if the system is stated outside of time.

We have pushed our analysis into domains which many philosophers regard as quite prickly and unresolved. Although our argument has not been presented with great subtlety and precision – we have leaned on analogies and images which might not withstand close scrutiny – the principles we have articulated are, we think, a natural and reasonable approach both to language and to the mind that contains it. In fact, we think an indirect approach to mind is perhaps the best approach. Certainly the most interesting mental phenomena are the capacity of human beings to have emotions, to dream up fantasies, make inventions, entertain paradoxes, etc. These capacities, however, are so thoroughly mental that they lack a consistent form of output to which we can apply rigorous analysis. Human language, however, is a mental product and has a number of very particular, exact features that are true of all speakers. A close analysis of language may therefore lead us to see principles which, in turn, may enable us to crack the deeper mysteries of the mind.

6. *The Organization of Phrases*

Social Science and Determinism

Marxist theories of revolution claim that a number of conditions must be present before a revolution will occur. The conditions are diverse: they involve political, economic and social unrest, as well as climatological, military and geographic factors. Revolution occurs when these factors interact in the consciousness of a population.

Marx's theories were based on many concrete observations. They have been upheld by subsequent events as well; and they have provided the basis for a great deal of scholarly work in the social sciences. In fact, Marx himself claimed that this theory was 'scientific' in character because it involved the objective analysis of concrete phenomena. He claimed the virtue of being 'scientific' precisely because his observations had a basis in objective reality rather than in subjective impressions.

In this sense, his use of the term 'scientific' was legitimate; in another sense, his theory of revolution, like many in the social sciences, is not scientific. It fails to be scientific because it is not deterministic. One can point to many social situations where all of Marx's objective criteria for revolution are met but where no revolution has happened. Therefore something crucial is missing in the analysis. What is missing is a specification of a *mechanism* that makes the various factors interact. The mechanism may obey principles of its own.

We might gather the ingredients of a cake and still not have a cake – it must be mixed and cooked just so. Or we might pile up the parts of a watch and still not have a watch. Observing that a watch has hands, jewels, bendable metal etc. is like observing the objective conditions needed for revolution. Unless one can state how the parts connect, one cannot guarantee that a watch will work or that a revolution will happen.

It is not clear that there is a specific mechanism behind revolutions, but there is definitely a mechanism within watches. And it follows what we can call a principle: the bendable metal is shaped into a spring that unwinds at a controlled rate. Many current watches, of course, are built on different mechanical principles, but with essentially the same result. Different mechanisms can produce the same outward behaviour.

It is the mechanism – and its principles – which makes a theory scientific because it gives us absolute rather than probabilistic knowledge. We can assert with certainty that a properly built watch will work. If not, there is always an identifiable problem.

It is popular in some quarters to approach psycholinguistics as Marx approached revolution: by listing the crucial ingredients, but without stating the mechanism whereby they interact. In fact Piaget is known for his view that language is an 'interaction' among mental faculties. There can be little doubt that this claim is correct, but it is far from the whole story. From our perspective, the essence is missing: the *mechanism* of interaction.

Principled and Haphazard Interactions

The study of language processing must solve two puzzles at once: what are the ingredients, and what mechanism makes them interact. These problems compound each other because one can make some astoundingly incorrect guesses about a mechanism if one is unsure of what parts are being coordinated.

Understanding and Producing Speech

How could such problems arise? Suppose we were to observe that mouths and ears serve three functions: speaking, hearing and eating. Now suppose that you were given only the information that there were three orifices that fulfilled these three functions. Suppose further that you could not see faces and watch what happens where. This situation is precisely what we have with respect to the inside of the mind. We cannot see what goes on in the brain while we think, so we must conjure up the mechanisms involved by using our knowledge of what the mind can do, coupled with a little bit of physiological information about the brain.

So now we have three functions and three orifices. The first natural guess might be that each orifice served a different function. One for hearing, one for speaking, and one for eating. It is difficult to talk and listen at the same time, and it is difficult to talk and eat at the same time, but it is possible to listen and eat at the same time. These are the kinds of empirical observations we might make about behaviour. Based on these observations, we might invent a mechanism that closes one orifice when it opens another. The eat-orifice would close the talk-orifice, and the talk-orifice would close the listen-orifice (and vice versa). We could carry our artificial example of 'science' much further, but some basic points should be clear.

1. It is possible to build a mechanism that approximates reality but is in fact completely misdirected.
2. The actual mechanism may be quite surprising: two orifices are used for hearing (ears), and one is used for both talking and eating (mouth).
3. It is the mechanism and not the components which is the central puzzle, but unclarity in one domain can lead to unclarity in another.

There are events in the world for which there is no mechanical explanation. If two cars come around a corner

118

and crash, then the motion of each can be explained mechanically, much of the crash itself will have a mechanical explanation, but the fact that both cars were there at once may have no mechanical explanation. It will be an 'accident' which resulted from a set of probabilistic factors: people deciding for independent reasons to drive to places will sometimes drive to the same place. The 'law of averages' predicts that such events will occur, but no coordinated mechanism is guiding those two cars to the same place at the same time.

There is the same potential for 'accidents' in the use of language. If I say a sentence and stop at the end of the sentence, then the place where I stopped is predictable by the theory of grammar. If, however, I stop because someone shoots me, then the place where I stop will not be predictable on linguistic grounds. It can be anywhere in the sentence.

All of this should seem very obvious. We can, however, extend the problem into nonobvious domains quite easily. If, while I am talking, I suddenly realize that I need to turn off the stove, I might interrupt myself. If my interruption is not predictable by the grammar, then it will happen anywhere. But if I continue to the end of a phrase in a systematic fashion before turning off the stove, then we might be able to assert that self-interruption followed a mechanical principle: it is only permitted when a particular language task is complete. Now we are stating exactly how two cognitive faculties – saying a sentence and thinking about unrelated things – could interact mechanically. Of course we know that there is a systematic interaction between thoughts and language because we put thoughts into language during the process of speaking. It's not a perfect process. Hence, we must experience many 'ums' and 'ahs' before the meaning comes through. We have been considering another question: how do *irrelevant* thoughts affect the speech process? We have concluded, just by thinking about it, that there might be a systematic interaction.

Click Experiments

There are some relevant experimental findings, however. Fodor, Fodor, Garrett and Lackner (1974) presented subjects with sentences on tapes in which there was an extraneous click in the middle of the word *company*:

> As a direct result of their new invention's influence the company was given an award.

The reader might feel that this sentence needs a comma after *influence*. That feeling reflects our knowledge that the noun phrase *their new invention's influence* ends at that point. The click was not placed at that point but rather on top of the word *company*. (One sound track is laid on top of another.) After the subjects heard the sentence, they were asked where the click had occurred. They answered, to a significant extent, that the click had occurred just where we would put a comma (after *influence*).

In other words, they literally heard more than one thing at once. The click was as irrelevant to the sentence as some errant idea popping into one's head. Their minds, however, registered the events in serial fashion, one after another. What defined the boundaries of one thing? It was not the end of the sentence but one of the invisible boundaries in a sentence – the end of a phrase. This shows that there is a capacity for the coordination of disjunct mental faculties. The interaction was not random but mechanically adjusted to allow the completion of the phrase. In addition, this lends credence to the claim that the invisible phrase boundaries are 'psychologically real' – they are needed not just to describe language in intellectual

120

discussion, but rather they function in the split-second computations of the mind.

Modularity

The notion of 'interaction' is captured in current linguistic work through the term **modularity**. The term suggests that disjunct mechanical modules interact to produce the surface of language behaviour. Both their internal structure and their systematic connections need to be understood.

Our mouthwork imagery can be enlightening here too. Suppose we knew that mouths dissolve food, but we could not look inside them. Every once in a while a stray wet tooth emerged from the mouths of children. The strength of the tooth might lead us to believe that it was sufficient to pulverize food. Some organic faucet to make it wet would also be needed. What would ever lead us to the hypothesis that in addition to the teeth there is a tongue that has a strong muscle in it for the manipulation of food? It would be a hard hypothesis to uncover, but suppose we arrived at the conclusion that there is a tongue. What is the relation between the teeth and the tongue? Together they dissolve food, but one responds to jaw muscles and the other twists and turns with its own muscles. We can slip our tongue in and out between our teeth without chopping it off, but otherwise the two muscles do not show the kind of tight interaction that exists between hand and arm. If we were to try to describe the teeth and tongue as a single system we would be led to many wrong notions of the mechanism involved. It is crucial to separate the two systems – the two modules – and seek the principles that govern each before we seek a description of how they interact.

Are all mental abilities necessarily modular? This view is not excluded, but one might seek to distinguish integrated systems from fully modular ones. J.A. Fodor (in press) mentioned the following example of how certain kinds of systems allow integration with general knowledge. If I am your friend and I point a gun at you, you might not worry about it because you know I am your friend. However, friend or foe, if I wave my hand right in front of your eyes, you will blink. That is because blinking is a reflex action, it does not take into account that a nearby object comes from a friendly source. One meaning of a reflex action is that it is a response to a specific stimulus. We cannot integrate large amounts of diverse information into the decision apparatus. Our entire personalities may be involved in our decision about whether or not to flinch when we see a gun, but no part of our personality or experience will affect whether or not we blink. Therefore, in a sense the *blinking* is modular in a way that the *flinching* is not. Nevertheless the flinching may also involve the coordination of a number of basically modular abilities, just as the tongue and teeth are both modular and coordinated.

This discussion is once again rather close to common sense. It is extremely important, though, because science can suffer decades of pointless research if people look for principles in the wrong places. The history of science is full of attempts to find principled accounts of human nature in what turned out to be hopeless places. From astrology to phrenology to, in our opinion, behaviourism, scientists have sought to elevate small correlations to the status of principled explanation. Such fields tend to die out when progress in them ceases. We must be careful in linguistics and psycholinguistics because language has connections to many parts of mental life. One might easily try to account for two separate abilities within the same system, when no single system exists. Let us consider one further example.

It is clear that human beings can set words to music and create songs. Our phrasing suggests two systems. However one might take the view that language contains music and that therefore we are looking at a single system. In fact, sentences are spoken with an intonation pattern that has certain musical properties. There is definitely a set of connections between the way ordinary language is spoken and musical structure. The connection has been explored recently in various studies of intonation (e.g., Liberman and Prince, 1977).

At the same time it has been observed that musical ability is not equally distributed in the population, that it may in fact be localized in a different part of the brain, and that it may be used independently of language. Thus, we have good evidence that separate systems are involved; but it is not clear where the line should be drawn. Maybe musical ability enters directly into intonation. Maybe the intonation system is separate from music in its mental representation, but simply seems as if it is musical. And maybe aspects of our musical ability are duplicated in language ability but represented separately. Thus stereoscopic vision and stereophonic hearing appear to work on the same principles but seem to be represented separately in the brain.

With respect to syntax, we may not always be sure if we are describing phenomena in our grammar that belong in a parser, or if there is a syntactic effect that is not really the result of an independent cognitive ability. In a word, a science can be quite advanced but still be unsure that it knows what it is talking about.

One might now ask: what tells you if you know what you are talking about? The answer is really circular. It must make sense, but not just 'common sense', rather *mechanical* or, we might say, 'principled' sense. Then we have good reason to believe it. If our concepts of elementary sentence and noun phrase show up repeatedly in different domains of grammar, and if we can specify a mechanism (like our *loops*, developed above), then we have a coherent domain in which we can believe. Highly coherent domains are regarded as systems and are then a natural source for hypotheses about neural structure.

They are natural sources but not necessary sources. It might be the case that we are dealing with highly misleading epi-phenomena. The systems could be mathematical generalizations that have no biological meaning. However, it is natural to believe that a highly structured system cannot be accidental and therefore must have a distinct representation in the brain that corresponds to the representation in the mind that we have developed. The brain is a physiological object while the mind is a philosophical object. Therefore it is, in general, appropriate to represent the mind in nonphysiological terms. Nevertheless, the ultimate representation of the brain will include the mental representation but with an explicit statement of its concrete (physiological) manifestation.

Interpolations

It might turn out that some features of language do not actually belong to language. For instance, when we interrupt ourselves, we do not always maintain the grammar we have initiated:

> John – just a minute the telephone is ringing – could you get the coffee.

The 'just a minute' part is an interpolation. It is reasonable to say that it is another completely different sentence that has nothing to do with the outer sentence. When it occurs is, on the whole, arbitrary. But it represents an interruption of the language system by the language system, so we still seem to be in the language system. Still, *when* the interruption occurs seems to be determined by a completely different system, namely, the auditory awareness that the telephone is ringing. The principles of interpolation may not be entirely linguistic in character, but they may have a very weak sensitivity. For instance it is unlikely that interpolations will occur inside phrases.

Unlikely: The – just a minute the telephone is ringing – man arrived.

Or within words themselves:

Unlikely: Sup – just a minute the telephone is ringing – per is on the table.

(See Clark and Clark, 1977, who discuss the question, giving a summary of some research on the topic.) Our tendency is to allow such interpolations to occur, but to begin the words and phrases again once interruptions have passed:

Sup – just a minute the telephone is ringing – supper is on the table.

Needless to say, however we decide to represent interpolations, our on-line processor must be able to identify them. Otherwise it would not be able to make sense of it all.

Conjunctions

Our discussion has been aimed at the problem of what the boundaries of a coherent system are. We have suggested that the boundaries of grammar may not lie at the edges of language, but somewhere within language. For instance **conjunctions** appear to have very little impact on sentences and their principles in most cases:

John arrived late, but Mary arrived on time.

Mary arrived on time, but John arrived late.

The *but* links the two sentences, but it seems to have no particular effect on the structure of those sentences. It must occur outside of each of them:

*Mary arrived but on time, John arrived late.

We get ungrammaticality if we put the *but* in the middle of a sentence. We might then make the suggestion that the system of *conjunctions* lies altogether outside of grammar. The fact that they are expressed as words does not mean that they are a part of grammar. They may be a part of a larger system but fail to interact with any of the principles of grammar. They could be direct manifestations of our cognitive faculty for logical relations. In fact, many conjunctions are logical in character: *unless, and, if ... then, only if, or, not,* etc.

This line of reasoning illustrates the idea that the boundaries of language and of grammar, strictly defined, might be quite different. However, this particular claim requires examination and, in this instance, turns out to be false. Conjunctions do interact with the principled aspects of grammar; and, therefore, we will be unable to exclude them from the grammar:

John ate fish, and Bill —— ham.
What John liked —— but Bill hated —— was fish.

In the first of these two sentences we see that the conjunction permits deletion of the verb, *Bill ham*, while in the second, the conjunction allows wh-movement to occur. Thus the *what* is both the object of *like* and the object of *hate*.

The inquisitive reader will notice that sentences like the second will not be easily processed by our HOLD mechanism. The *what* will be dumped out after *liked*; and, when the *but* clause arrives, the sentence will require reanalysis in a special way that allows us to make the two sentences *John liked* and *Bill hated* stand in parallel so that they will receive the same object. They must have *exactly* the same object; if it is *fish* Bill hates then it must be *fish* that John likes and not *meat*. This will require an extra mechanism which we shall not discuss, primarily because it has not been dealt with very satisfactorily in the processing literature. (For an interesting linguistic analysis, however, see Williams, 1979.)

We have seen that the isolation of mechanical principles requires that we have an accurate notion of exactly what territory the mechanism should cover. In the case of language it remains partly unclear what territory is covered by grammar, what is covered by a processor, and what is covered by other cognitive faculties. The answers are not known beforehand. It is by the success of the postulated systems themselves that we decide where the lines must be drawn.

Lexical Ambiguity

Two systems which interact but must be kept separate are the structural system and the lexical system. The lexical system is the dictionary or vocabulary we have in our heads. It is full of idiosyncratic facts and oddities of meaning which do not resolve into a rule-governed system. At the same time, it contains a number of morphological rules. For instance, we can add *-ness* to any adjective and generate a noun: *strange* ———→ *strangeness*.

One reason that it is necessary to separate lexical structure from syntactic structure is that the two produce different kinds of ambiguity:

> After the right turn, John laughed.
> After the left turn, John laughed.

127

These two sentences have identical syntax, but one is lexically ambiguous while the other is not. The first sentence contains the word *right* which can mean either the 'direction to the right' or 'correct'. In most contexts ambiguities are resolved by neighbouring words, but in some contexts they remain ambiguous. They provide another factor that makes the comprehension of a sentence more difficult.

Other ambiguities are purely structural:

John carried a book for Susan.

All of the words here are unambiguous, but the phrase *for Susan* can be seen as a part of the noun phrase *a book for Susan* or it can be a part of the verb phrase *carried for Susan*.

The two systems can also be linked. The choice of verb can dictate the structure chosen:

John selected a book for Susan.

Here the verb meaning *select for Susan* is chosen. The only difference lies in the verb *select* which strongly prefers a so-called benefactive prepositional phrase (*select for Susan*). Among the verbs that are ambiguous, the ambiguities do not all have equal weight:

John organized a book for Susan.

Here the benefactive *organize for Susan a book* seems to be the preferred reading, while the noun phrase *a book for Susan* is less likely but still possible.

We can even find our preferences for attachment operating on the basis of such unlikely factors as popular television culture:

a.   I saw the programme with Bill.
b.   I saw the programme with Bill Cosby.

The latter sentence is likely to be parsed as *the programme with Bill Cosby*, i.e., as a single complex noun. The former is much more likely to be parsed with the phrase *with Bill* modifying the verb *saw* (*Bill and I sat in the living room and watched a programme on TV*). Perhaps if you were Johnny Carson speaking, the same reading would be just as likely for the second sentence (if Bill Cosby is a friend of Johnny Carson). This comment is meant to be facetious, but it has a very real point. Extra-linguistic context can also play a role in how we make linguistic decisions.

Here we must tread carefully. We have enlarged our domain of relevance to include many things outside the language sphere – and yet we can see that their effects are real. In the discussion that follows let us keep one task in mind: how will we distinguish the principled interactions from the haphazard interactions?

Just how does the processor function in a domain where so much is relevant? We have seen that with respect to gaps, the processor will make a 'standard' choice, then reanalyse when it has obviously made an error. Now we may ask the same question with respect to the analysis of sentences where there is no gap: what is the 'standard' choice without lexical or contextual influences?

Late Closure

Is there a 'standard' way to determine where a phrase ends? Let's see if we can deduce an answer to this question. How is the word *yesterday* most naturally interpreted in these sentences?

a.   John said Bill died yesterday.
b.   Mary planned to become a nurse yesterday.

Understanding and Producing Speech

In (a) the preference is for the reading that Bill died yesterday rather than the reading that John said it yesterday. In the next sentence the *yesterday* associates most naturally with *Mary planned*. This is because it is semantically quite odd to use the futuristic expression *to become* with respect to the past. If we had instead *Mary wished Bill had come yesterday* then the *yesterday* quite easily associates with *come*. In order to establish what the standard association is, we need neutral examples. Consider:

a. John saw Bill jump yesterday.
b. Fred made Sam sing yesterday.
c. Mary thought Bill sang last week.
d. Fred dreamed Mary was elected last week.

The predominant interpretation seems to be that *yesterday* or *last week* associates with the second clause, or in these instances, the subordinate or lower clause. Now, is the association just with the lower clause or is it with the nearest clause? We can once again do a linguistic trick to find out. If we reverse the order of the sentences, the preferred readings change:

a. Bill sang, Mary thought last week.
b. Mary was elected, Fred dreamed last week.

Now the *last week* associates with the main or higher clause, which is also the nearer clause. It is proximity and not subordination that seems to determine what the standard association for temporal adverbs is. Lyn Frazier (1978) has identified and dubbed this phenomenon **late closure**. When one is processing a sentence, we can conceive of it as having an opening and a closing bracket.

$$[_S \qquad\qquad]$$

When one starts a sentence a bracket is begun:

$$[_{S_1} \text{ John thought } [_{S_2} \text{ Bill died } \ldots.$$

Now we have started two sentences and finished neither. When we get to the word *died* we could finish S_2 and leave *yesterday* outside:

$$[_{S_1} \text{ John thought } [_{S_2} \text{ Bill died } _{S_2}] \text{ yesterday } _{S_1}]$$

If we did, then *yesterday* would belong to *John thought*. The concept of late closure means that we include as much as we can inside a sentence before we close it off:

$$[_{S_1} \text{ John thought } [_{S_2} \text{ Bill died yesterday } _{S_2}] \, _{S_1}]$$

Note that the entire S_2 falls inside of S_1, which is what it means to be a subordinate clause. The *yesterday* is clearly a part of the lower S_2 clause. Once again we can see the processor manipulating the invisible boundaries provided by the grammar. The late closure principle says that we should include as many incoming constituents as possible before adding the second sentence bracket.

The late closure principle can, in some instances, complicate our expectations:

John put the book that Mary had been reading in the study.

This sentence is odd at first because we feel that another phrase is needed. This is because *put* requires a locative phrase. We cannot say **John put the hat*, but rather we must say something like *John put the hat in the drawer*, where a locative is provided. However the sentence has a locative, so it should cause no problem. The phrase *in the* *study* fulfils the requirement of *put*. This is quite true, but what we seek to explain is this initial reading – the half-second of noncomprehension when we look for another phrase and none is there. The late closure principle predicts this state of affairs. The phrase *in the study* is first seen as part of the relative clause sentence [*that Mary had been reading in the study*], and then one must reanalyse and close the sentence earlier, leaving *in the study* to fulfil the locative requirement of *put*: [₁ . . . *put the book* [₂ *that Mary had been reading*₂] *in the study*₁]. The very fact that our principle predicts interactions of this subtlety is evidence in its favour.

We have looked at how the mental machine divides up the ends of sentences, but we have not asked how it deals with the beginnings. Let us construct some examples where the grammar generates certain structures but the parser seems to balk. Note first that the following contrast exists:

a. That Bill is here is good.
b. *Bill is here is good.

The problem with the second sentence is that we do not know that the first phrase *Bill is here* is a subordinate clause. If we add a *that* in front it is like a signal that the sentence following is not the whole sentence but just part of a sentence. How does the mind represent this fact? There is evidence that the mind regards such subordinate clauses as a part of a noun phrase. The following sentence has just the same meaning:

It is good that Bill is here.

The *it* seems to refer to the whole sequence *that Bill is here*. We can represent this claim by saying that a sentence is inside a noun phrase: [NP[S]]. Such a structure is obviously more complex than just a sentence: [S]. Therefore the *that* is like a signal to put the sentence inside another set of brackets.

Now, there is something curious about this *that*. In the sentence **Bill is here is good*, the absence of *that* makes the sentence ungrammatical, but *that* is freely deletable when the clause comes at the end:

> It is good Bill is here.

Why must it be present at the beginning of sentences but not when the clause comes at the end? The answer lies not in the grammar but in the demands made upon the parser. When the *that* comes at the end, the parser already knows what the main clause is; and it already has a tell-tale *it* for which a referent must be found. The grammar then connects the *it* to the following clause and automatically assigns the structure [$_{NP}$[s]]. In other words, just when the *that* is redundant in determining the structure of the sentence is it also deletable.

Redundancy

We may now ask how we should formulate this parsing restriction. There is a long tradition in biology, and also in linguistics, of grabbing at the notion of *redundancy* and using it as a pivotal concept in the construction of a theory. The trouble with this approach is that it is vague. There is no meaning to the term 'redundancy' unless it is defined with respect to a particular task or theoretical construct. Are two tables in a room redundant? Not if there are two people at work at them. (Or is the second person then redundant, too?) If we are able to define redundancy precisely with respect to a particular construct, then we can dispense with the term altogether.

Even with a particular theory, we must be careful. We have sentences of the form *The girls hit the boys* and *The boy hits the girls.* There are two ways to determine that the subject is plural: it is marked on the noun by *-s* for plural and on the verb by *-s* for singular. Why should it be marked on the verb if it can be determined by reference to the noun by itself? The phenomenon of **noun/verb agreement** in fact provides unnecessary 'redundancy' in language, but (unlike *that*) it is not optional. Some people attribute this to the imperfections of language. We suspect that there is an explanation at some deeper, currently unattainable, level of analysis. There is some coordinating function of the verb marking which we do not yet understand. We are like people from another planet who, upon finding a dead man, wonder why he has two legs instead of one. There must be some explanation for agreement because it is present in so many of the world's languages. It is the kind of puzzle which is currently a topic of study in linguistic theory.

If we wish to avoid allusion to 'redundancy', how can we explain the obligatoriness of *that* in clause-initial sentences? Let's think again about how we *misunderstand* the incorrect sentence: *Bill is here is good.* The problem quite obviously is that we take *Bill is here* to be the main clause. In other words, we project a structure like [s] instead of [np[s]]. Now we are in a position to state another principle:

Never project more structure (brackets) than you have specific evidence for.

The *that*, then, provides specific evidence for another bracket at the beginning of the sentence. When the subordinate clause appears at the end of the sentence, when a main clause has already been projected (*It is good* ...), one is forced to project something other than a main clause. The presence of *it* invites us to produce an [np[s]] structure. If one wants to project another main clause, then we need another specific signal: *and*. This leads to a totally different construction of the sentence under review: *It was*

134

good and Bill was here. Now the *it* must refer to something specified by context or by a previous sentence.

In general, specific words — nonreferential words that don't point to anything in the world — point instead to parts of sentential structure we carry in our heads. As a general guide, we follow the mechanical notion that every extra word signals an extra piece of structure. This has the right kind of mechanical properties to be a plausible principle to pursue. The reason we say 'pursue' is that language is so complex that it is not immediately obvious whether the principle is correct. Therefore we adopt it and see how far we can make it work.

Structures inside Structures

There is another peculiar thing about how *that* works. We have already established that the human mind can tolerate lots of repetition — lots and lots of repetition. There is very, very, very much of it. But if we come up against a sentence like the one below, our whole apparatus seems to go haywire:

> That that that Bill was here John suggest you had the idea was good.

We can unpack this sentence just the way we did before, and it comes out quite comprehensible:

> It was good that you had the idea that John suggest that Bill was here.

The problem cannot simply be that there are too many *that*s because in other circumstances we tolerate repetition. It must be that there are too many of whatever *that* stands for. We have said that the *that* signals our putting one structure inside another. Therefore the string of *that*s

135

means a string of brackets, and that is what makes the sentence difficult to comprehend.

How can we state this restriction in a way that is mechanical and not vague? And what is the deeper intuition behind it? Let's look a little more closely at the phenomenon:

That that John sings was known is good.

This sentence is borderline for many people. A similar one definitely is passable and occurs a good deal: *Who who came late will leave early?* In real life, intonational factors further improve such sentences and make them far more frequent than you might think.

We can also improve such sentences by choosing transparent semantics for them: *That that Kennedy was shot was broadcast everywhere was never decided upon by the networks.* However we have no mechanical way to state the notion of 'transparent semantics'. We will return to the question of where semantics should fit into our account, but we will continue to seek a statement of the phenomenon that is limited to those things which are mechanically definable.

Suppose we say simply that a subordinate clause cannot be processed while one is in the middle of a subordinate clause. This notion can be generalized: no structure can be processed while the same structure is being processed. These formulations may be too strong, but they appear to be in the right spirit. They may be too strong because we have just shown that it is just about possible to handle sentences with two *that*s occurring together, while total impossibility seems to emerge when three *that*s appear. The facts are a little fuzzy.

One might retort that this fuzziness undermines the analysis. Can something fuzzy arise from something mechanical? The notion of a mechanism seems to imply absolutism and determinism. A moment's reflection would

136

reveal that this view is merely a prejudice. A record with dust on it can be fuzzy, but of course the dust is not part of the mechanism. The braking system of the car is very gradual, but its gradualness is the purpose of the system. In fact when two different mechanisms interact, some fuzziness is frequently the consequence. The interaction is still mechanically specifiable.

Suppose now a second mechanism is involved: memory. The grammar generates these triple *that* sentences. We cannot stop it from doing so if we allow a sentence to occur in a noun phrase. Wherever a noun phrase occurs, a sentence can occur. This inevitably produces triple *that* sentences. However, we might place a limit on memory that states, in effect, that extra memory is needed if an organism tries to carry out an operation while it is in the middle of the same operation (Miller and Chomsky, 1963). In other words, it is hard to start a clause when we are in the middle of another clause. Being 'hard' does not mean it's impossible or that the grammar should rule it out.

This view has the advantage that it states a relation between two mechanisms: the system that generates sentences and the processor which has to remember what it's doing while it does it. However there are straightforward counterexamples to what we have said. If I say that *the man in the moon just arrived* I have put one noun phrase, *the moon*, inside another one, *the man in the moon*. By the time I get to *the man in the* I have started another noun phrase before finishing the first one. Yet we detect no great difficulty with phrases of this sort. We must then find some other way to differentiate the problem *that* sentences.

Notice now that we can sometimes use a double *that* sentence with no ill effects: *that that man came is good*. We do not have a borderline sentence just because there are two *that*s. The reason is that the second *that* is a demonstrative – not something that introduces a whole sentence, just something that picks out a particular man (we can label it *that*$_N$). The consequence of this fact is that the parser not only may be dealing with a structure inside an identical structure, but that it may not be. The word *that* is ambiguous between a sentence introducer and a demonstrative. In other words, the parser is unsure at the beginning if it has *that*$_S$ *that*$_N$ or *that*$_S$ *that*$_S$. So it cannot right away make an absolute decision about what structure it is dealing with. Note that one possibility can be automatically ruled out: *that*$_N$ *that*$_N$. This is because there is no possibility of saying something like *I like that that man*.

The parser is not unsure when it deals with ordinary noun phrases, in general, because it has already established the existence of the noun phrase when the second noun phrase inside it begins (as in *the man in the moon*). There are some noun phrase situations where ambiguities arise and they, putatively, cause some difficulty as well. We have two analyses for: *I saw the man with the telescope.* Either *the man with the telescope was seen by me* or *the man was seen by me with a telescope*. The problem here, intuitively, is substantially less because the range of alternatives at the end of the sentence is smaller. The basic structure of the utterance is already established.

Let us try to summarize what we have seen so far. Structures inside structures, which we can call *self-embeddings*, cause problems. The problem seems to be one of memory and not of grammar. The problem is confounded if the parser cannot be sure if it has to unravel an embedding or not.

There are some other structures that lend support to this view. For instance, if we are exposed to the following sentence, we can swiftly determine that it is nonsense:

The rat the cat my mother bought bit died.

It is all right to put a bare subordinate clause inside a main clause: *The cat my mother bought died.* But if a subordinate

138

clause is inside another subordinate clause, the system cannot cope.

Note that in fact the analysis of the first three nouns given above is not the only possible one in this situation. We could have said *the rat, the cat, my mother and my brother all went to the store*. Here the nouns are conjoined as the subject of a single verb, rather than being the subjects of different verbs. In addition, we find that semantics can shift the acceptability of such sentences. For instance, *The socks the girl I like bought are nice* seems to be much easier to understand. Thus along several dimensions we have evidence that our principles are correct and are susceptible to the same kinds of exceptions.

Structure and the Systematic Lexicon

We have discussed two purely structural principles: late closure and self-embedding. Each of them operates with concepts provided by the grammar but refers to the effects of time – the actual process of comprehending a sentence.

We have avoided speaking of lexical effects because they must be integrated into the model very carefully. Let us begin with the most explicit phenomena. We know that verbs carry structural information with them. At the most primitive level there is the distinction between transitive and intransitive:

       a.   John slept.
       b.   *John slept his arm.
       c.   Bill upset the basket.
       d.   *Bill upset.

Intransitives may not take an object, and transitives require an object, although semantically it might be quite

139

plausible to use an intransitive transitively. For instance, *John slept his arm* could mean *made his arm go to sleep*.

A verb like *put* requires a structural locative phrase – as we remarked before. It is possible to say *I put it away/in the cabinet/here*, but it is not possible to say **I put it beach* because, although *beach* is clearly locative, the requirement is a formal one. We can represent those formal requirements by creating a dictionary entry in the mental lexicon that has empty positions for required materials:

$$put \text{ [NP] [PP]}$$

The empty phrases must be filled, or the sentence is ungrammatical: **I put the ball*. It is not merely nonsensical. We can prove this by saying *I put health in the oven*, which is a pretty nonsensical sentence although it is completely grammatical. These are the tests that show us that we are dealing with a mechanical phenomenon. In other cases it is sometimes difficult to say if we have a formal mechanism.

We said earlier that the principle of *late closure* will overrule our expectations for a sentence like:

They put the book that the girl was reading in the study.

We expect another locative phrase because we first see the phrase *in the study* as part of the lower verb *reading*. Where do our 'expectations' come from? They come from our knowledge of the verb *put* which requires a locative. The same expectation is not present for *see*: *I saw the girl who was reading in the study*.

It is important to point out that these are not loose, vague, personal 'expectations' but inevitable expectations based on the structural character of the lexicon.

Difficult Reanalysis

Sentences which we are forced to reanalyse are called 'garden path sentences'. Our first analysis turns out to be faulty so we have to backtrack – we've been led down the garden path. There are garden paths that have severe consequences – they put us in a perceptual jam that is hard to escape. Ford, Bresnan and Kaplan (1983) have noted cases like the following:

> The boy got fat melted.

While the problem with the *put* sentence lay in the fact that we needed further information (a locative), this sentence gives us extra information. *The boy got fat* is fine by itself, but what do we do with *melted*? Some readers will conclude that this sentence is nonsense. The fact that such readers exist shows that 'reanalysis' does not necessarily continue on tirelessly *ad infinitum*. At some point we give up – we accept noncomprehension rather than searching any further. That point will certainly vary from person to person – it is not a part of the reanalysis mechanism.

Other readers will reanalyse until they discover a reading where *fat* is a noun, as in *the boy got the fat melted*. Why is this reanalysis so much harder than others? The explanation lies partly in a simple mechanical fact. This is unlike the problem with prepositional phrases, where we had to decide which verb the prepositional phrase belonged to. Here we must change the *category* of a lexical item. The word *fat* can be either a noun or an adjective. The verb preceding *fat* can take either a noun or an adjective: *John got angry* or *John got bread*. Note that in the sentence *John got fat meat*, the adjective *fat* belongs to the noun *meat*, not the previous verb *get*. But since in both cases *fat* is an adjective, this reanalysis is easy.

We now have a correlation, which is something less than an explanation; but it is a good place to begin looking for

141

one. If we must reanalyse the syntactic category of a word, then substantially greater perceptual difficulty occurs. Why should category reanalysis be more difficult than reorganizing the association of phrases? One involves only a single word while the other requires juggling a whole bunch of words. Obviously, however, number of words is not the right measure of difficulty. What we must do is construct a theory that predicts the differential difficulty of two kinds of analyses.

The first observation is that we appear to have evidence that the analysis of phrases is independent of the analysis of words, or at least the analysis of words into their 'part of speech' (word class). Suppose we make an assertion and see if it works out right. A perceiver first identifies words and assigns them to syntactic categories or 'word classes'. Then he bundles them up into phrases and decides how the phrases should connect to each other. If there is a problem, he tries to reassociate the phrases in a different way. If there is still a problem – no analysis is satisfactory – then he must dig deeper into his original assumptions, into his initial word-identification, and seek to find alternative categories for the words themselves. Digging deeper causes greater difficulty.

Now in fact a lexical entry is more complex than we said. Consider *want*:

$want_V$	NP	*He wants cake*
	NP to V	*He wants Bill to go*
	to V	*He wants to go*
$want_N$		*His wants are numerous*

The $want_V$ is listed with the subsequent phrases that it can take. The perceiver is ready for any of them (or ready to switch among them) as new phrases come in (i.e., *he wants cake*, *he wants to go*, and *he wants Bill to go*). If he hears *he wants cakes to go* it is not too difficult to decide that this is a case of *want NP* because *cakes to go* is a unit, and the phrase means something like *he wants take-out cakes*. However, to switch category from verb to noun is much more difficult. In our model it means moving from one part of the lexical entry for *want* to a different sub-entry altogether. If we hear *School wants are less important than home wants*, we have a hard time making the transition from verb to noun in the first phrase (*school wants*). It is interesting that, once done, the analysis is easily available for the second phrase (*home wants*).

In this fashion we can construct representations that match our intuitions of perceptual difficulty. Are we constantly bothered by such difficult reanalysis? Hardly. The grammatical system prevents these ambiguities in most instances. We find that *the* or *to* generally tells us what is what: *I began to run* or *I began the run*. Nevertheless, though rare, difficult sentences give us insight into the organization and ordering of information in split-second mental computations.

Summary

We have discussed four principles that a parser uses. Two of them involve the pure manipulation of phrases: late closure and self-embedding. The other two refer to formal aspects of the lexicon: syntactic category and empty phrases associated with particular verbs. All of these principles are weak reflections of meaning differences. It may be no accident that *try* is a verb and *sugar* is a noun, but many words can be either (*the run* or *to house*). Nevertheless, the system has a formal character which allows the parsing system to operate rapidly and efficiently. Most of the real meaning of words is ignored. Our parsing principles can be aware that *put* and *find* both take locatives (*find a tack here*), but the principles make no reference to the fact that *put* means something totally different from *find*. We could make the whole system work using completely artificial or nonsense words. Lewis Carroll did just that with his nonsense verse, 'Twas brillig and the slithy toves did gyre and gimble in the wabe.' Moreover, there are computer programs which can – to some degree – successfully undertake the parsing of sentences in terms of these formal principles. They have none of the human awareness of the real meaning of words.

We have quite obviously been avoiding the impact of the real meaning of words throughout this discussion. In occasional asides we have observed that 'transparent semantics' makes certain analyses easier. What we will do next is to look at how the other aspects of meaning – those which resist formalization – affect parsing. We have sought to make a strict division between the two kinds of meaning because we believe they belong to separate parts of the mind which are, however, brought to bear on the same phenomenon: understanding sentences.

Our point of view is not shared by everyone in the field of psycholinguistics. There are those who advocate a 'completely interactive' system where all parts of the mind are involved in a single mechanism for analysing sentences. We think that there are separate domains which appear to be intimately connected, but which really have limited points of contact. Furthermore, we are not sure that their interaction lends itself to a mechanical description at all. But we are getting ahead of ourselves.

'Real' Meaning

Some verbs, like *give*, carry two incompatible pieces of structural information. They are incompatible because they both convey the same meaning. The receiver is expressed in two different ways, either *I gave Bill the money* or *I gave the money to Bill*; but they cannot be used both ways at once: **I gave him the money to Bill*. In other words, we can represent the lexical entry for *give* with two lines of empty slots which can be filled in when the verb is used in a sentence:

give   [NP] to [NP]
         [NP] [NP]

The parsing question that arises, of course, is this: which structure is one using when just one noun is present? If I have a sentence that begins *I gave the baby* I could finish it either by adding *a sandwich* or I could add *to the doctor*. In one sentence *sandwich* is the object and *baby* is the recipient. The parser does not know which structure will be chosen when just one noun is present; but, on the other hand, the parser does not have to wait long to find out. The next word (preposition or NP) will reveal the choice.

There are sentences where the choice is far more obscure. Suppose I said *Who did I bring the patient?* This could mean either *I brought the doctor a patient* or *I brought the patient a doctor*. Which do you think is better? There is little doubt that both are possible, as we can see if we change the objects: *Who did I give a sandwich?* or *What did I give Bill?* Where does the wh-word come from, the first or the second NP position?

Is it wh verb NP *X* or wh verb *X* NP?

The answer does not seem to hinge upon anything in the structure of the sentence – it hinges instead upon the exact content of the words. *Sandwich* is unlikely to be a recipient, while *Bill* is unlikely to be the object given. When we make parsing decisions in terms of the content of individual words, however, we rapidly lose our grip on a mechanical procedure. Why? Because the choices are often less clear than the examples we have given; the parsing decision must then wait for an analysis of the entire context, plus perhaps the personalities of the conversationalists in question. Imagine a cannibal who feeds people to

145

animals saying *Who did I give the dog?* It might mean *I gave the dog John (to eat).* From the mouths of the Humane Society the parsing would work differently.

It is clearly possible to make parsing decisions in terms of specific lexical items (as we have seen and will see), but there is an interesting fact about the sentences we have just been discussing. In a number of dialects, and perhaps everywhere, there seems to be a general preference for interpreting all such sentences as having the wh-word coming from the position right next to the verb, or next to a preposition. Thus *What did you give to Bill?* is fine and *Who did you give a present to?* is, too. In each case there is absolutely no ambiguity about where the missing NP is. It will work even if the sentence is complete nonsense: *What did you donate to a table?*

We are witnessing two very interesting and fundamental linguistic phenomena. On the one hand, the parsing system is open to contextual and lexical influence, while on the other hand, it seems to be trying to close off that domain because it is rife with uncertainties. The preferred readings are in league with a mechanical determination of how parsing should function. Lexical variation is being avoided.

Why isn't lexical variation completely avoided? There is a paradoxical answer to this question, which has to do with the powerfully mechanical nature of language. The grammar says that nouns should be extractable from verb phrases. Therefore a rule necessarily exists that will take the noun out of a structure like *V noun noun.* The rule cannot say to itself, 'Do not do this operation if ambiguity will result.' Nevertheless ambiguity results if we do not know which noun has been taken. Therefore a kind of filter of 'comprehensibility' keeps most speakers away from sentences of this kind, but the filter cannot be built into the grammar itself.

In other words, the system wants a mechanical and nonlexical means to interpret sentences. Apparently the lexical system that allows a double-object structure is not entirely sensitive to the transformational system. The transformational system will extract one of the nouns even though it cannot reliably provide the hearer with information about which one has been extracted. This task is then left to general inferences that try to make speech comprehensible. In other words, since the grammar and its parser are formal mechanisms, we cannot build knowledge of the whole world into them. This is one of the consequences of saying that the grammar is both modular and mechanical in character.

Which Parts of Meaning are Formal?

Our representation of the word *give* with two lines of syntactic context is partly responsive to the meaning of the word *give*. The concept *give* naturally involves the transfer of objects between people. This aspect of the meaning of the word receives, apparently, a formal representation in terms of a sequence of possible phrases that we can put into the lexicon as we did above. Other aspects of the meaning of *give* receive no formal representation. The notion of generosity associated with the 'act of giving' is not explicitly represented anywhere.

Why not? Is this an accidental characteristic of English? It is difficult to answer these questions in an absolute fashion. It is true that grammars sometimes encode rather odd aspects of a particular culture. In Hopi there are affixes that represent different kinds of motion. In other languages there are affixes that represent whether or not one has witnessed an event. In Japanese there are honorific affixes that encode subtleties of social interaction. So it is difficult to assert that we could not have an affix that means 'done generously'. On the other hand, it seems safe to say that the languages of the world find formal ways to say a set of typical human meanings. Thus most languages have declaratives, questions and imperatives, because apparently people like to state, ask and command. And languages typically like to have a particular form – like the double-object construction – *I gave John candy* – to represent the recipient and object together.

We have no answer to the deeper question of why languages have a formal mechanism for some purposes and quite variable, context-dependent general inferences (or knowledge) for other purposes. A deeper understanding is necessary before we can answer these questions. A first step toward answering them lies in providing an exact account of what is within the formal mechanism of language and what lies outside. By 'outside' we do not mean completely outside but rather limited to special places – inside the meanings of words or as a comprehensibility check on the output of a grammar and a parser.

Charades, Freud and the General World of Inferences

We are trying to forge a path between two kinds of meaning – although we are not sure what the boundaries should ultimately be. Let's try to move ourselves to one extreme: a completely nonformal synthesis of word-meaning. Many people who hear the following sentence are quite nonplussed:

This book fills a much-needed gap in the literature.

It sounds like typical dust-jacket gab. Others burst out in laughter: those who laugh parse the sentence correctly. It is apparently not the *book* but the *gap* which is much-needed. For those who see the sentence as sensible, a different kind of word-calculus has transpired. They must have felt that *much-needed* associates most naturally with *book* and not with *gap*, so they put them together mentally.

148

They could not put them together syntactically because there is no syntactic transformation that will switch an adjective from inside one noun phrase to the inside of another.

Is this kind of association weird or unnatural? Suppose I said *Look for a book next to a red boat*, and you looked around at a variety of sailing gear and suddenly saw a red book next to a boat. Something inside might suddenly say, hey, this must be it – the right ingredients are present. However the guess would be wrong even though the right ingredients are there. Well, what's going on?

We know that people associate meanings with life, not just words. The meaning associated with life is not just the sum of perceived objects. If we see someone with a knife in their back and someone else is running away, we might (courageously) follow instantly in hot pursuit. We have made an inference about what transpired. It could be wrong: the runner might be a passing jogger unconnected to the crime. But, clearly, we are mentally equipped to make inferences of this kind. Similarly, when we play charades we try to determine the nature of a set of words; but we do not use syntax to arrive at a meaning. Or if we analyse a sentence as involving a Freudian slip, we are analysing jointly both the sentence and our knowledge of the personality in question in an effort to establish something about the world. The point is that sentences and words are themselves objects in the world to which people can apply normal inferences.

The analysis of the *much-needed gap* suggests that this process is largely independent of syntax. It operates over and above – or sometimes against – what the syntax is saying. The syntax takes a bunch of words and associates them in one way, while many ways may be possible. The inference capacity of human beings associates them in a completely different way, trying, usually, to find the most 'natural' interpretation for them in a given context.

Most of the time, inferences and syntax arrive at the

same result. This is what enables one person to finish another person's sentence. He has guessed not only what the syntax requires but the rest of the meaning as well: *I didn't think I needed to tell you* ... (other voice): ... *that he will leave right away*.

This has led some researchers to seek an exact point – an opening – when inferences will be brought to bear upon the processing of a sentence. They can, after all, be very helpful in guessing beforehand which of several possible empty phrases a person will use.

Consider a famous sentence in this regard:

The horse raced past the barn fell.

The last verb is quite jarring – it has no home. A very slow reanalysis of this sentence will lead most speakers to the realization that the meaning is really *The horse which was raced past the barn fell*. It is so natural to think of the horse racing by itself that one does not automatically think of the fact that *horse* could be the object of a hidden passive verb phrase. The verb for *horse* is really *fell*. The inference is applying immediately, making us choose one of two possible readings. If we had instead the following sentence: *The horse selected by the manager fell*, we could easily arrive at just the syntax (a hidden passive) that was so difficult to reach in the other sentence. Examples like these make one think that inferences are central to the parsing process. Nevertheless, we think that they are not.

Let us consider a further example:

I chose the boat floated down the river.

This sentence is not so difficult, but not so easy, either. A temptation remains to see *the boat floated* as an active sentence and not a reduced form of *the boat which was floated*. The fact that this inference survives is very important. The word 'survive' is not ill-chosen. The early

150

part of the sentence involves the word *chose*. We can say
I chose a box or *I chose to sing* but we cannot say **I chose
that Bill sings* on analogy with *I believe that Bill sings*.
Therefore while it is possible to say *I believe the boat floated
down the river* we cannot say such a sentence with *chose*.
This means that the parser ought to be limited to just a
noun phrase. A noun phrase can have a passive within it:
the man chosen is here. The phrase *the man chosen* is a noun
phrase by itself functioning as the subject of the sentence.
In the sentence *I chose the boat floated down the river* the
parser, when it gets to *I chose*, knows that (barring the
appearance of infinitival *to*) a noun phrase and not a
sentence must follow. Therefore when it gets to *the boat
floated*, the parser should automatically, without regard to
inferences, impose the passive reading on the phrase. This
does not happen. Therefore, the inference capacity seems
to be operating without regard for the dictates of syntax
(just as in the *much-needed gap* case) discussed above.

We are led to the following conclusion: inferences
operate everywhere.

In other words, they do not have a principled interaction
with the formal properties of grammar; they have a
haphazard interaction. They work whenever there is
sufficient information to justify an inference. It can happen
that a person stops within a word: *I knew th...*, and
another person says *that you would be late*. He might not
have inferred the remainder of the sentence if it had not
begun with *th*: *I knew a*. Here a noun phrase and not a
clause would occur. The inference capacity took the sound
th, plus knowledge of the situation, and inferred the entire
contents of the clause.

It is demonstrably the case that inferences will alter
preferred attachments, even if they hinge upon something
as small as a definite article. Frazier (personal communication) points out that we get different readings for the
following two sentences depending on whether *the* or *a* is
used:

    a.   I hit the man with a hard hat.
    b.   I hit the man with the hard hat.

In the second sentence it is difficult to assume that *the hard hat* is the instrument, the thing with which you hit the man, while in the first sentence this is a natural interpretation. Of course, what is natural in a neutral context can be overturned again by biasing the context. If there is a particular hard hat under discussion – then one might say *I hit the man with the hard hat* and get an instrumental reading. If there is no hat present, the use of *the* serves as a way of identifying which man one means from among many.

If, as we say, inferences are everywhere, then there must be an oversupply. Indeed, since inferences can build upon inferences, there are potentially infinite chains of inferences associated with every word in a sentence. How? Well, suppose someone arrived and said 'beer'. He would, we might infer, be thirsty, be over the legal drinking age, be familiar with Western culture, be unafraid of making demands, perhaps be disinclined toward polite vocabulary, etc. These inferences are not necessarily true, but neither are any other inferences. The consequence of all this is that every sentence should, in principle, generate many unwanted inferences.

It is unclear how many of these unwanted inferences are subconsciously generated and subsconsciously rejected, but it is clear that most hearers have few of them left when they arrive at the end of a sentence. One natural suggestion is that the syntactic limitations function as a filter on possible inferences. Therefore only those permitted by the syntax will in fact surface. This suggestion seems to be in the right spirit, but it is clearly too strong. Examples which we mentioned earlier would be ruled out under this hypothesis. It would not be possible to misunderstand *this book fills a much-needed gap* if inferences were unable to travel paths that seem to be closed off by the syntax. We

152

are left then with the conclusion that inferences operate with few constraints, but that somehow most incorrect inferences are rejected in the light of syntactic information.

If there are two mechanisms interacting, then a rough conclusion may be the only conclusion. Greater precision may be impossible in describing these two systems. Substantial efforts have been made in trying to relate these phenomena in a principled way, but it may be that they belong to those inquiries that are doomed by the way they formulate the problem. Note that we are talking about the interaction of inference and grammar. It may well be that inferences themselves are highly principled, although the issues are not yet very refined. There is a substantial philosophical literature on the nature of inferences.

Inferences: of What are They a Part?

It may sound ironic, deceptive, or at least paradoxical to say that inferences are extremely important to successful parsing but that they are not a part of parsing. Here we have to seek a special kind of conceptual clarity. We might paint a stove black and declare that the colour is part of what makes the stove beautiful. And yet, though the paint is everywhere, we still might want to say that the paint is not part of the stove. Our reasoning has to do with the special nature of principled discussions. Only the principles count; everything else has to be seen as a separate system – a separate module. A principled account of a car would make reference to the engine and wheels but not the seats. A car could exist with a stand-up driver. A seat, though present in all cars, bears no principled relation to the engine or the wheels. Remember that we are constructing a theory of parsing. Theories are not natural objects; nothing extraneous is permitted in them if they intend to be a set of principles. Natural objects virtually always

153

constitute a set of partly connected and partly extraneous phenomena.

We are saying in effect that, because inferences are everywhere, they are nowhere in our theory. Obviously, anyone who wants to deal with an aspect of language must acknowledge the role of inferences. This acknowledgement can take the form of an *account* of how inferences in fact interact with parsing mechanisms, but an *account* is not a theory. In reality an account of how inferences and parsing interact may be extremely important – perhaps more important than our theory. It could be, for instance, that a child exhibits some language deficiency because for some reason he fails to do inferences at the same time that he listens or reads. Teachers of reading often bemoan children who read without being aware of what they are reading. The fact that they can do so testifies to the idea that parsing and the comprehension of sentences are separable, which is of scientific interest but of no help to the child.

We have come full circle. The reason we dwelt on the distinction between principled and haphazard interactions at the beginning of this chapter is because we believe that it is crucial to the understanding of the mechanical aspects of language. It is wise to point out, though, that the issues we have discussed do not really submit to the kinds of glib and easy-going analysis which we have presented. They involve issues of great philosophical depth which remain less than fully resolved. There are those who believe that no coherent principles underlie language. There are those who believe that there are no 'real' principles at work in the universe. For them, our theories are quirks of the imagination that fit part of the known evidence but never encompass all of the evidence. We have tried to use the notion of modular interaction as a means to predict the fact that theories never cover *all* of the facts, just part of the facts. However there are those who believe that the problems with human theories come from the inadequacies and biases of the human mind. They believe we are not equipped to understand the world we live in in any ultimate terms. They believe our theories are really no more than sophisticated rules of thumb for navigating through life. Needless to say, we are more optimistic about the strengths of science. Though much of the world may remain forever mysterious, science can gain genuine insight into some things.

What kinds of things resist human understanding? It may be that analysis fails where human will is involved. Whatever it is that falls under the name 'motivation' is something for which a deep understanding may remain forever elusive. Because the human will is involved in inferences (you hear what you want to hear), it may be that we will never arrive at an understanding of how inference works in a way that is comparable to our understanding of how parsing works. On the other hand, perhaps inferences involve several subparts, and we can subdivide the problem just as we have done with parsing. These ideas remain sheer speculation until careful work on human inference (currently underway) gives us a better sense of its dimensions.

Where Do Sentences Ultimately Go?

What happens to sentences after they are finished? What are we left with when the conversation is through? There are those who argue that every sentence spoken is recorded and is somewhere in an unconscious memory. There are examples of great mnemonists who appear to have word-by-word recall of every conversation they have had (like the fictional Archie Goodwin in Rex Stout's stories). Nonetheless it is clear that most of us are not left with sentences, nor are we left with nothing. Rather, something called the 'gist' of what was said is available for conscious recall.

How does the brain get from a sentence to the 'gist' of a sentence, and when does the 'translation' take place? As usual this offhand version of what minds do hides a host of tricky technical questions. We can try to refine the question by looking at some simple examples. Most people would prefer the first sentence below to the second.

> The group lost its leader.
> The group lost their leader.

The reason is that *group* is grammatically singular, though it refers semantically to a plural. Often, people who prefer the first sentence above will accept the sentence below:

> The group followed a long path through a forest and then travelled for many miles before realizing that their leader was drunk.

The plural reference *their* is more acceptable when it is somewhat distant from the noun (*the group*) to which it refers. Why? One natural explanation is that the hearer and the speaker have already translated the noun *the group* into a form in semantic memory where it is a plural, and the fact that it was once grammatically singular is forgotten.

Is this a haphazard business? Do we get our ideas out of grammar as fast as we put them in? Or do we keep the grammar in mind for a certain length of time? It is certainly necessary for us to keep it in mind for a certain period, otherwise we would find a good deal of ungrammaticality in everyday speech that seems not to occur:

> *The group which yesterday appeared to be on the verge of a decision, now act otherwise.

We remember that a subject is singular across a rather

lengthy noun phrase: *group* and *act* must agree, so we need to say *acts* to make the sentence grammatical.

There is, however, evidence that many other aspects of the syntax of sentences can disappear. If asked immediately, a person will know that the second sentence below is not a repeat of the first:

> Bill hit John.
> John was hit by Bill.

But if one allows a few minutes to elapse after saying 'Bill hit John' and then asks, 'Did I say "John was hit by Bill"?' most speakers will no longer remember if the original sentence was in the active or the passive. The sentence has been translated into some other level of mental meaning. In fact, the words themselves disappear. If I say *Bill shoved John*, and ask you three minutes later if *Bill pushed John* you will probably say yes. We would regard the person as pedantic who said, 'No, he *shoved* him.'

It is a matter of some interest about mental meanings that meaning relations are not always bi-directional. If I say *John yelled at Bill yesterday about the meeting* and then ask *Did John talk to Bill about the meeting?* the answer would be 'yes'. But if we begin with the assertion *John talked to Bill yesterday about the meeting* and then ask *Did John yell at Bill about the meeting?* the answer would be 'No, he just talked to him'. Why the difference? Apparently the notion of *yell* includes the notion of *talk* inside it, but not vice versa. We cannot *yell* without talking, but we can *talk* without yelling. It will clearly not be adequate to claim that we have a mental representation of meaning that is in words.

This view seems a bit jarring to those who believe fervently that we think in words, but there can be little doubt that we do not think in words even when conversations are what we are thinking about. If we consider other domains of mental activity, the role of words seems

157

even more remote. When a halfback races down the field, dodging oncomers left and right, he must do a great deal of mental computation (including awareness not only of how muscles move but of the rules of the game). It is hard to imagine that all of this activity is carried out in words. And if, after the game, we ask him why he leapt to the left, he may struggle to find the words that will formulate what was a clear thought in his mind. Obviously, the thought was not in words in the first place.

How long is long-term memory? The question is an impossible one. It can quite clearly be as permanent as a human being himself. The person who remembers that 'as a child my mother always told me to be kind to crickets' has translated a few sentences into a life-long memory.

One can, however, do research on the question of how fast information gets translated into long-term memory and what kind of information is present. In fact there is a long tradition in psycholinguistics of pursuing this question. We have not and will not pursue these questions in depth because they require an introduction to issues of methodology which are too laborious. In any case we believe that the essential issues are evident intuitively and do not require detailed experimental explanations.

One common hypothesis (see Fodor, Bever and Garrett, 1974) is that the clause boundary is the point at which sentences are translated into a nongrammatical semantic mode. If sentences are translated into the realm of ideas, then all the words may be abandoned as well. Perhaps we are left with just an image as a rather economical way to remember things. Of course this is far from obvious. What is the image for a sentence like *John is a nice guy*? Here are a couple of experiments that try to tackle this issue.

Caplan (1972) gave people the following two sentences of roughly equal length with the word *rain* appearing in the middle:

158

When the sun warms the earth after the rain, clouds soon disappear.

When a high-pressure front approaches, rain clouds soon disappear.

The word *rain* belongs to the first clause in the first sentence, but it belongs to the second clause in the second sentence (*rain clouds*). Subjects were asked to identify the word *rain* as part of the sentences one second after each sentence was said. Caplan's prediction was that for the first sentence, since the first clause is long finished, the word *rain* should already have been shipped off to long-term memory. Therefore it should be harder to identify as being part of the sentence. In the second sentence *rain* in *rain clouds* is part of the clause just finished, therefore it should be quickly available. In fact, recognition time was significantly faster for the second sentence as compared to the first. This provides clear evidence for the claim that the sentence boundary has an effect on memory, and it is consistent with the theory that we begin to translate sentences into a nonlinguistic mode even before they are complete.

A subtle experiment that may show how we use images in memory was performed by Bransford, Barclay and Franks (1972). Subjects were given the following two sentences, which differ only in the prepositions *on* and *beside*:

Three turtles rested *on* the floating log, and a fish swam beneath it.

Three turtles rested *beside* the floating log, and a fish swam beneath it.

Three minutes later, the subjects were given the following sentences and were asked if they were the same sentences they had previously heard:

159

Three turtles rested on the floating log, and a fish swam beneath them.
Three turtles rested beside the floating log, and a fish swam beneath them.

The sentences differ only inasmuch as *them* is substituted for *it*. However, subjects believed that while the top two were the same, the bottom two were different. That is, they thought that *three turtles rested on the floating log and a fish swam beneath it* means the same as *a fish swam beneath them*. In fact the meaning is slightly different, but one meaning entails the other. If you swim under the log you will necessarily swim under the turtles, too. In the other sentence, where the turtles are *beside* the log, you will swim under different things if you swim under *it* or *them*. It is clear from the results that the subjects were not sensitive to whether the pronoun *it* or *them* was used, since in the first instance they thought they had heard the *same sentence*, but they are sensitive to meaning differences based on two different mental images (the image of swimming under a log or under turtles or under both).

Conclusion

We have sought to show how a wide range of different factors can be at work in the virtually instantaneous subconscious process of sentence processing. They include not only context but personality, personal experience, and whatever else makes our minds alive in so many ways at once. At the same time we have sought to show how a set of mechanical principles embedded in this process exists for the purpose of providing a skeletal analysis of syntactic structure. We have tried to indicate where we think interactions are haphazard and where they are principled.

One ulterior goal has been to illustrate how the scientific

quest can both use common-sense intuitions about our experience and lead us to conclusions quite foreign to common sense. Since much of the crucial data comes from within ourselves – our intuitions of what is grammatical and what is difficult – we can see the whole scientific process in a microcosm. We can see how theories illuminate new questions and how we can address those questions by creating relevant examples. The examples can then be tried out by running them through our own language processors.

Another ulterior goal has been to demonstrate in detail why the human mind is a marvel and why it remains mysterious. The great step forward in linguistics, once again, lay in the realization that it is the creativity with which we use language that must be explained. A recognition of human creativity in the linguistic sphere suggests that we should seek it elsewhere as well. There is no reason to think that humans are not just as emotionally, morally and aesthetically creative as they are linguistically creative. And the creativity of which we speak belongs not just to the artist or the leader but to every human being that speaks, feels, judges or admires.

7. Producing Sentences

In a sense, producing sentences is just the reverse of comprehending sentences. In comprehension we take a string of sounds and work back to the message intended by the speaker. In production we start with the message and work forward to a string of sounds that will carry our message to our listener. The processes involved in the production of sentences, however, are probably not simply the same as those used in comprehension but applied in the opposite order. There are special problems which confront the speaker which do not affect the listener. For example, the speaker must choose his words, not merely identify them; and he must also plan the syntactic structure of his sentence, not merely recover the structure implicit in a string of sounds and words. Both the speaker and the hearer use the same knowledge of vocabulary, morphology and syntax (i.e., they share the same grammar); but speakers and hearers put that knowledge to use in different ways. Thus, both the speaker and hearer are recruiting the same knowledge, but the mechanisms that make use of this (shared) knowledge are probably different.

It isn't easy to study sentence production because we are handicapped by our inability to do controlled experiments. It is relatively easy to do experiments on sentence comprehension because we can systematically manipulate the input to the sentence comprehension mechanisms. That is, we can present our subjects with various kinds of sentences to process and measure things like 'processing load' and the time it takes to understand the sentences. But it is hard to see how we can manipulate the input to the

162

sentence production mechanisms. The input to the sentence production mechanisms is a *message*, and how can we control what messages our subjects in the laboratory will choose to express? This problem is not insurmountable. We can, for example, ask our subjects to describe pictures or the actions depicted in little movies and thus gain some control over what our subjects will talk about. But we cannot systematically manipulate other critical variables like what syntactic form our subjects' sentences will take and what words they will choose to put in their sentences. (However, see Osgood, 1971, for some interesting experiments in this area.)

These difficulties in systematically controlling the input – and output – of the sentence producer have led most researchers who are interested in sentence production to do studies that are, for the most part, *observational* in nature. In particular, researchers have focused on various departures from ideal speech such as hesitations and various kinds of speech errors like 'spoonerisms'. The hope is that by looking at the ways in which the sentence production process can go awry we will be able to gain some insights into the mechanisms that are involved in producing sentences.

Hesitations

We have already said a little bit about hesitations and what they reveal about sentence structure. Here we will concentrate on what hesitations – or nonfluencies – reveal about what goes on when we are putting together a sentence. There are basically two kinds of hesitations that we can find in speech: silent pauses and so-called filled pauses (*ums* and *ahs*); and much of the research that has been done has examined the relation between the occurrence of such hesitations and various linguistic variables.

The first thing to note about hesitations is that they tend

to occur in places where subjects must 'stop and think' about what they will say next. Goldman-Eisler (1958) showed that pauses often precede a sudden increase in the information being communicated. This 'increase in information' was estimated by seeing how easily subjects could predict the next words of a sentence when they were given the part of the sentence that preceded an observed pause. Tannenbaum, Williams and Hillier (1965) have also shown that pauses tend to occur before words that are less predictable by the preceding sentential context. Thus, it appears that hesitations are often found in places where the speaker must make a choice.

Hesitations do not always coincide with phrase or sentence boundaries, although syntactic structure is clearly a factor in determining where hesitations will occur. Maclay and Osgood (1959) showed that hesitations were related both to phrase boundaries and to places where speakers made decisions about what words to use. That is, we find hesitations in places where people must choose what structure to use next and in places where they must choose what word to use next. Interestingly, Maclay and Osgood found that filled pauses (*ums* and *ahs*) tended to occur at phrase boundaries and that silent pauses tended to occur within phrases where lexical rather than structural decisions are probably being made. Within-phrase hesitations occur most often before content words (nouns and verbs, for example) (Martin, 1967), which indicates that these pauses are related to speakers' word-finding difficulties. Maclay and Osgood took this as evidence for the existence of two distinct levels of organization involved in sentence production: a lexico-semantic level and a syntactico-grammatical one. Thus, evidence from hesitation phenomena leads us to postulate at least two levels of organization for speech production and gives us some indication that speech is planned ahead of time, since it appears that speakers occasionally take time out to think about what they are going to say next and how they are going to say it.

Speech Errors

If pauses indicate places in sentences in which speakers stop to think about what to say next, then it appears that speakers plan their sentences before they utter them. We have already noted in Chapter 3 that the existence of certain kinds of speech errors – or slips of the tongue – suggests that speakers plan significant portions of their sentences before uttering them. The mind, then, is in some sense ahead of the mouth during speech production. The question that arises immediately is how far ahead of the mouth is the mind. A major source of evidence about the structure of the plans that speakers make before uttering sentences is the study of errors that speakers spontaneously make in normal conversations. This area has been given a fair amount of attention in recent years (see Fromkin, 1971, 1973, 1980; and Garrett, 1975, 1976); and much has been learned from this study. Careful analyses of speech errors have led some researchers like Garrett (1975, 1976) to propose models of sentence production in which there are a number of different levels of planning.

We will describe Garrett's theory a little later on, but first let us have a look at the kinds of speech errors that are commonly found. The examples here are taken from the UCLA corpus (Fromkin, 1971), the MIT/Cornell corpus (Garrett, 1975), and from a small corpus of errors collected by one of the authors (EM).

Exchanges. One of the common errors found in speech occurs when two linguistic elements switch places with one another. The classic examples are so-called spoonerisms in which words or parts of words are exchanged. Thus, for example, *the dear old queen* becomes *the queer old dean*. Exchanges occur at all linguistic levels, from words and phrases to morphemes to sound segments to phonetic features. Here are some examples:

WORD EXCHANGES

... but a *beach* on the *bikini* is all right.
(Intended: *bikini on the beach*)

Other things would *expect* us to *lead* that ...
(Intended: *lead us to expect*)

Older men *choose* to *tend* younger wives.
(Intended: *tend to choose*)

MORPHEME/SYLLABLE EXCHANGES

He favours *push*ing *bust*ers.
(Intended: *busting pushers*)

That book by Norm*el* and Rum*an*hart ...
(Intended: *Norman and Rumelhart*)

SOUND SEGMENT EXCHANGES

Marmosets li*p* sac*k* from trees.
(Intended: *lick sap*)

That's what *T*omsky was *ch*alking about.
(Intended: *Chomsky was talking*)

We will go down to the sound *r*oof *pr*oom.
(Intended: *sound proof room*)

PHONETIC FEATURE EXCHANGES

... the *gl*ear *pl*ue sky ...
(Intended: *clear blue sky*; the voicing features of the

166

initial consonants of *clear* and *blue* have been ex-changed)

Shifts. Shifts occur when a fragment of one word gets attached to another word in the speech sequence. These errors often involve the 'movement' of a suffixal mor-pheme, as the examples below show.

SHIFTS

They get weird ever*ier* day.
(Intended: *weirder every day*)

No one quite know what*s* to do with it.
(Intended: *knows what to do with it*)

Anticipations. Sometimes parts of a word which will be coming later in a sentence appear as parts of an earlier word. These errors are different from shifts because the parts don't appear to move, they merely are 'copied' on to an earlier word.

ANTICIPATIONS

Wenatchie is the app*ital* capital of the world.
(Intended: *the apple capital*)

I'd like some smo*y*ked oysters.
(Intended: *smoked oysters*)

Perseverations. Some errors are like anticipations, but the influence of one word shows up on a later word in the sentence, as these examples show:

PERSEVERATIONS

Take your feet out of the stirrups and wallop him in the ch*ollops*.
(Intended: *wallop him in the chops*)

167

I'd like a cup of co*pp*ee, please.
(Intended: *cup of coffee*)

Other errors. There are many other kinds of speech errors; but they are, on the whole, not relevant to the study of sentence production. We mention a few here just for the reader's interest. *Malapropisms* occur when someone uses an incorrect word in place of a correct one. Most of these errors resemble the right word in terms of number of syllables and stress pattern. These errors are often intentionally used for comic effect, as with Sheridan's Mrs Malaprop (from whom we get the name) and with the character of Archie Bunker from the American television show, *All in the Family.*

MALAPROPISMS

She went to the *groinocologist.* (*All in the Family*)

We need a little something to break up the *monogamy* around here. (*All in the Family*)

Long ago, I laid my positive *conjunctions* on her never to think on the fellow again .... (*The Rivals*, Sheridan)

We will have more to say about malapropisms in the next chapter.

We also find *blends* in which two words become mashed together. Classic examples of these are Lewis Carroll's 'portmanteau words' like *slithy* (*lithe* + *slimy*). Some examples that have been observed in spontaneous speech follow:

BLENDS

Nobody gets very *upcited* about that. (*upset* + *excited*)

I don't like your *insinuendos.* (*insinuations* + *innuendos*)

168

Finally, we find what might be called *semantic errors* in which the wrong word is chosen. In cases like these, the error is usually a word that is closely associated with the target word in meaning (*nurse* pops up instead of *doctor*) or is the opposite of the intended word in meaning (*Open the door* instead of the intended *Close the door*). The classic examples of this kind of error are the 'Freudian slips' (Freud, 1974, 1975). An example of this kind of 'slip' comes from a professor who Freud observed to remark:

> In the case of the female genitals, in spite of many *Versuchungen* [temptations] – I beg your pardon, *Versuche* [experiments] . . . .

Such classical Freudian slips are quite rare, however; but they occur often enough to elicit the raised eyebrow and knowing smile from the true connoisseur of the Freudian slip.

What Can Speech Errors Tell Us?

Observing the foibles of our fellow speakers can be quite interesting and often amusing, but we entered into this discussion with a purpose. We want to know what we can learn about the processes that underlie sentence production from errors like the ones we have discussed. It turns out that it is most instructive to look closely at what we have called exchange errors.

Notice first that exchanges occur between elements that appear in similar environments. When words are exchanged they are often in similar syntactic positions (*a bikini on the beach – a beach on the bikini*). When segments or syllables are exchanged they come from similar positions in the words: *pushing busters, lip sack, Tomsky was chalking*. The exchanged items are also similar: words exchange with words, syllables with syllables, and seg-

169

ments with segments; so the errors occur only between items that are described on the same linguistic level. We never find exchanges which involve elements from different linguistic levels; for example, words do not switch places with sound segments. This is evidence for the existence of different levels of description for utterances, and they appear to be exactly those levels which linguists talk about. It is also interesting to note that word exchanges *tend* to occur between words of the same part of speech. Nouns tend to get switched with nouns, verbs with verbs, and so on. A similar constraint shows up with sound exchanges. Consonants exchange places with other consonants, and vowels switch with vowels. Only rarely do we find a consonant switching with a vowel or vice versa; and when we do find such exchanges, they occur between adjacent sound segments.

Nearly every investigator has also remarked on the extreme rarity of speech errors which result in violations of the constraints on sound sequencing in whatever language is being spoken. That is, we do not find errors which end up in 'illegal' sequences of sounds. Thus, for example, a possible error on the phrase *slips of the tongue* would be *tips of the slongue* but not *tlips of the songue*, since the combination of consonants *tl* is not a possible word-initial consonant cluster in English. Notice that such sequences are perfectly pronounceable; they are simply ruled out by the rules of English phonology. It appears, then, that there is some part of the speech production process that prevents such illegal sequences from coming out. It could be that there is some sort of 'low-level' editing process that picks out errors that violate the phonological/ phonetic sequencing constraints before they are uttered. Thus, the errors that we find are all *possible* words in English, or whatever language we are looking at.

Finally, we find that prosodic factors seem to influence the form that speech errors take. It has been clear for some time that exchanged elements share certain prosodic features, that of *stress level*, in particular. Exchanges between vowels and syllables occur between elements that have the same word stress levels; that is, if two syllables are exchanged they will be either both stressed or both unstressed. In word exchanges we find that the words which participate in the exchange have the same phrasal stress level. There is also some influence of stress level on the likelihood of word exchange errors occurring. Boomer and Laver (1968) reported that the majority of word exchanges which they observed involved words which bore the main stress in a major phrase group. Other researchers have observed the same things in their collections of errors.

To summarize, then, we find that we can make the following generalizations about exchange errors:

1. The exchanged elements occur in similar environments with respect to word or syllable positions or phrasal positions.
2. The exchanged elements are similar to each other phonetically, prosodically and syntactically.
3. Exchange errors will very likely involve words that receive the main stress in major phrasal groups.
4. The exchanges will yield phonologically/phonetically permissible sequences.

There are other generalizations that we can make about speech errors, some of which can be used to help us construct the beginnings of a model for sentence production. We will turn to some of these now.

We have already noted that exchanges occur between elements that are described on the same linguistic level. We can carry this a little further and make the assumption that if exchanges occur between linguistic elements then those elements must appear at the same *processing level*. For example, if two words are exchanged we will assume that both words were mentally available at the same time.

171

This could be used to argue for a level in sentence production at which words are inserted into sentences. Using evidence of this sort, a number of theorists have constructed what we might call 'stage theories' for sentence production. Merrill Garrett's (1975, 1976) theory is fairly typical, and it is the most detailed; so we will discuss it briefly here.

Garrett has proposed that speakers plan their sentences on a number of different levels, and he has provided motivation for these levels by pointing out different error types and the different kinds of constraints on these error types that can be found. Garrett's notion is that sentence production starts at what he calls the *message level*, where the speaker decides what he wants to say. The speaker then decides on what Garrett calls a *functional outline* in which the speaker decides on what words to use and what grammatical relations they will bear in the sentence. At the next level, the *positional level*, the speaker chooses a syntactic representation for the sentence, inserts the little grammatical morphemes, and inserts phonemically specified representations of the content words. This representation is then 'spelled out' in phonetic detail (*sound level*), and these representations are used to send instructions to the articulators for the utterance of the sentence.

Because different processes are involved at each of the levels, we find different kinds of errors showing up, and we find different patterns of interaction between errors produced at 'higher' or earlier levels and those produced at 'lower' levels. In going from the message level to the functional outline we find that it is primarily 'semantic' factors that are involved. It is during this mapping from the message to the functional outline that semantically based errors such as word substitutions (*open the door* instead of *close the door*) and blends (*upcited* from *upset* + *excited*) occur. Lexical substitution errors such as malapropisms probably also occur here. In going from the functional level to the positional level we find errors such as word

172

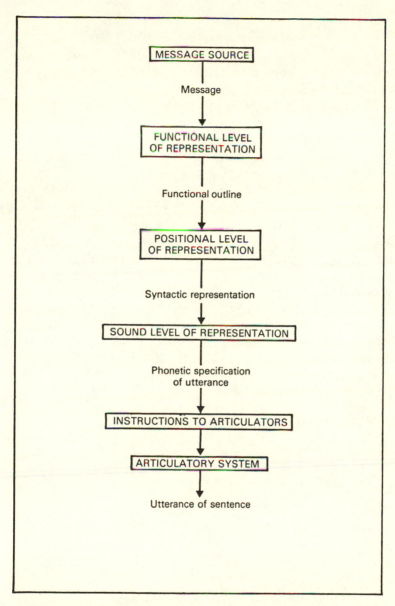

Fig. 7: A schematic diagram of Garrett's model of sentence production (after Garrett, 1976)

173

exchanges, morpheme exchanges, and word and morpheme shifts. Thus at this level we can get words or morphemes put into the wrong places. At the sound level we find sound segment exchanges like *lip sack* from *lick sap*. It is interesting to note that if words are exchanged, the distance between the exchanged elements is usually longer than that between the elements involved in a sound exchange. This suggests that the two levels are in some sense independent.

Further evidence for the distinction between the positional and sound levels comes from a class of errors known as *accommodations*. It appears that exchanges and word or morpheme shifts that occur at the positional level 'feed' the processes at the sound level. Remember that it is at the sound level that the phonetic detail of a sentence is specified. Thus, we find errors which indicate that errors occurring at the positional level are carried on to the sound level where the normal processes involved in spelling out the phonetic detail of a sentence are carried out. For example, we find that the form of the indefinite article will accommodate to its error-induced environment:

If you give the nipple *an* infant, then . . .
(Intended: *give the infant a nipple*)

a money's aunt
(Intended: *an aunt's money*)

We also find that the phonetic forms of tense and number morphemes are appropriate to the stems to which errors attach them, as in

roasted ([rəʊstɪd]) a cook
(Intended: *cooked* ([kukt]) *a roast*)

rodes ([rəʊdz]) pet
(Intended: *pets* ([pets]) *rode*)

add ups ([ʌps])
(Intended: *adds* ([ædz]) *up*)

And we also find that vowels are restored or reduced when a shift or exchange changes the environment of the vowel:

easy ([iːziː]) enoughly
(Intended: *easily* ([iːzɪliː]) *enough*)

It appears, then, that there is some level at which words and morphemes are chosen and inserted into syntactic structures (and at which they can be sometimes mixed up) that precedes the level at which precise pronunciations are formulated. The picture that emerges from all this is one in which sentences are planned at a number of different levels and in which some units of sentences are cognitively available earlier than others.

As with other topics that we have discussed, sentence production is an extremely complicated business; and we have ignored a whole host of factors that are undoubtedly involved with sentence production. The choice of a message and, to a certain extent, the syntactic form that the message will take, is governed by a large number of complex linguistic and cognitive mechanisms. Sentences, after all, are usually found in conversations or discourses; and there are many 'rules' which govern the appropriateness of sentences in these larger contexts. Osgood (1971) presents an intriguing set of experiments in this area in a paper called 'Where do sentences come from?' The reader can also consult Clark and Clark (1977) or Lyons (1981, this series) for more discussion of the interesting problems in discourse organization.

8. The Mental Lexicon

We have said many things about how we perceive and produce sounds and sentence structures, and we have mentioned a number of things that have to do with words and what we must know about them. For example, we have noted that a listener must have at his disposal information about such things as the part of speech of the words in a sentence as well as information about the sorts of structures that particular words can occur in. The processes involved in getting this information are usually looked upon as similar to those involved in looking up a word in a dictionary. The listener uses the phonetic or phonological representation of a word to 'look up' information about the word, its meaning, its part of speech, and the kinds of structures it can appear in. Until the listener has found this information in his mental lexicon he cannot go very far in parsing and understanding a sentence. That is, a listener must be able to get hold of information about the semantic and syntactic characteristics of words to help him comprehend a sentence. This look-up process appears to happen very quickly. A number of researchers have attempted to measure the time it takes listeners to get at this information, and they have estimated that it takes about 150 to 200 msec. to retrieve information about a word (Rohrman and Gough, 1967; Sabol and DeRosa, 1976). It is even possible to speed things up considerably without appreciably affecting comprehension (Foulke, 1971). The lexical look-up mechanisms, then, appear to operate very quickly and efficiently.

In this chapter we will try to do two things. First, we will collect the various observations that we have made about the kinds of information about words that language users must carry around with them in their heads; and then we will try to suggest how that information might be organized so that we can quickly and efficiently get hold of it.

What Do We Know about Words?

As we just mentioned, much of the discussion in this section will be somewhat repetitious. What we have said so far about what we must know about words indicates that the information which we carry around in our heads is similar to that contained in a standard dictionary. Obviously, the mental lexicon must contain information about how particular words are pronounced. This is essential for both speakers and hearers. A speaker must know how to pronounce a word once he has chosen it, and a hearer must be able to find information about a word's meaning, grammatical category etc. on the basis of its pronunciation. So, an entry in the mental lexicon must contain information about the *phonological structure* of the word. Because speakers and hearers are also, by and large, writers and readers, we would also expect to find information about the spelling of a word in its lexical entry. Because there is no one-to-one correspondence between sounds and letters in English, the mental lexicon must contain an *orthographic representation* for each word. For example, the sound that we represent phonetically as [aʊ] can be spelled in a number of ways: *cow, bough, fowl, foul* etc.; and the same sequence of letters can be used to represent different sounds: *cow, low, bough, bought, through.*

The mental lexicon must also contain information about the *lexical category* or part of speech of a word; that is, it must 'tell' us whether the word is a noun, verb, adjective or whatever. The part of speech of a word may appear to be predictable from the meaning of the word, but a little

177

study of the matter will reveal that the meaning of a word does not necessarily dictate its lexical category. If one looks at different languages one finds that words which *mean* the same thing, i.e., *name* the same objects, actions or processes, often have different lexical categories in different languages. The equivalent of the word *fire*, which is a noun in English, is a verb in Hopi (an American Indian language spoken in the southwestern USA). Other examples can be easily found; so it appears that the meaning of a word cannot be used to predict reliably its part of speech. Thus, we must assume that the lexical entries for words contain information about their part of speech.

Just as we cannot use the meaning of a word to predict its lexical category, we cannot use meaning to predict the kinds of syntactic relationships a particular word can enter into. Take the case of transitivity of verbs. Some verbs will take direct objects (transitive verbs), others will not (intransitives). This is not predictable from the meaning of the verb. Thus, there is nothing about the meaning of the verb *sleep* that would lead us to predict that the sentence

*John slept the bed

is ungrammatical. It is simply an idiosyncratic fact about the verb *sleep* in English that it is intransitive and does not appear with a direct object. It isn't hard to find other idiosyncrasies in the syntactic behaviour of words. Why is it, for example, that certain verbs like *believe* can take either an infinitival sentential complement or a tensed sentential complement while others, like *want*, allow only an infinitival complement?

He believes Hugo to be a liar.
He believes that Hugo is a liar.
He wants Malcolm to leave.
*He wants that Malcolm will leave.

178

Information about the kinds of syntactic structures in which a particular word can appear must, then, also appear in the mental lexicon. Such information is essential for speakers, if their sentences are to come out well formed; and, as we have noted above, this information can also be useful for hearers insofar as it gives them clues about what sorts of things to expect in a sentence after they have heard a particular word.

Certain exceptional features of words must also be represented in the mental lexicon. The majority of words in English undergo the regular morphological processes for such things as the formation of plurals (add -*s*) and past tenses (add -*ed*), but many words are exceptions to these regular processes. The plural of *mouse* is not *mouses but *mice*; the past tense form of *run* is not *runned but *ran*, and so on. Clearly, speakers and hearers must also have this information at their disposal.

It is also clear that it is not just words but also individual morphemes that must be represented in the lexicon. **Inflectional morphemes** like the plural -*s* and the past tense marker -*ed* are probably also contained in the lexicon, along with information about what sorts of words they can attach to, and what sorts of regular meaning changes they trigger in the words to which they are attached. It is also reasonable to suppose that the so-called **derivational morphemes** are represented in the mental lexicon. We have a variety of very useful little affixes that we can attach to words to make new words and change the grammatical categories of words: -*tion* can be used to turn a verb into a noun (*react/reaction*), *un*- can be used to reverse the action of a verb in some sense (*tie/untie*), etc. So it's not just words that appear in the mental lexicon but also all the various little morphemes that enter into the word formation processes in the language.

This pretty much exhausts the catalogue of things that lexical entries for words in English must contain, but some languages will have to contain even more information. A language like Latin, for example, will need to have certain kinds of grammatical information in the lexicon that English does not need. Nouns in Latin will need to have information about what declension they belong to; and verbs in Latin will have to carry information about which conjugation they are in. Languages with grammatical gender classes (like German or French) will have to have information about grammatical gender marked in the lexical entries for nouns. We could go on and on, but let's stop here.

It should be clear by now that the mental lexicon must contain quite a bit of information about the forms of words and their syntactic and morphological behaviour. All this will ensure that sentences will be well formed, that is, grammatical; but it does not tell us whether sentences will be meaningful or appropriate. Thus, along with all this information we must also have information about the meanings of words in the mental lexicon. How this information about meaning is represented in the mental lexicon (or if it is represented right in the mental lexicon) is a subject of considerable controversy. This is primarily because the study of meaning (semantics) is very difficult, and no one has been able to come up with a well-defined system for the representation of meaning that seems to capture adequately the notion that we have in our heads when we know the meaning of a word.

We shall not attempt to formulate a system for representing the meanings of words here (see Lyons, 1981, this series, for more discussion). Such a representational system will eventually have to explain all sorts of things. At the very least, it will have to explain how we can determine whether an utterance is true or false. It will have to explain how we can recognize that two words are the same or similar in meaning (synonymy), are opposite in meaning (antonymy), or are used appropriately in combination (the 'sentence' *the rock thought* is distinctly odd, for example). It must also capture what we know about the implicational structure of meanings: *John ran to the store* implies that John *went* to the store and, possibly, that John *intended* to go to the store. Somehow or other all these things and more will have to be accounted for in an adequate account of 'meaning'.

It is quite clear, then, that we carry around a substantial amount of information about each of the tens of thousands of words that we know. As we mentioned above, we can retrieve this information very quickly; and this leads us to ask how all this information is organized to enable us to gain access to it in an efficient manner.

How is the Mental Lexicon Organized?

Obviously, there must be some organizing principle or principles for the mental lexicon. The large dictionary on my desk would be just about useless if it simply contained a haphazard list of entries. The principle that is used in a standard dictionary is to list the entries in alphabetical order; so, if I want to find out about the word *empyrean*, I know approximately where to turn in my dictionary and can locate the information I need relatively quickly. If there were no organizing principle to my dictionary, I would have to start looking at the beginning of the dictionary and move along entry by entry until I found the word I was looking for. This would be a time-consuming and frustrating process if the word I was looking for didn't happen to occur relatively early in my search, and such a dictionary would be almost useless. There must be some sort of system for organizing such a large list of words and the information associated with them.

What, then, is the system that organizes the mental lexicon? It appears that the mental lexicon may be organized according to a number of systems. There has been a considerable amount of research in the area of 'lexical access', and it has been discovered that a number of different variables affect the speed of lexical access. This is perhaps not all that surprising because we have to get at information contained in the mental lexicon through a number of different routes. The problems which confront a listener, a reader and a speaker/writer are different. A listener must get at information about a word based on its pronunciation. A reader must get at information about a word based on its spelling. And a speaker must get at information about a word based on its meaning. What may be an efficient system for lexical access for a hearer might not be an efficient system for a speaker. Thus, it might make sense for there to be different ways to get at the information contained in the mental lexicon. (See Forster, 1976, for a review of research in this area.)

Now, what sorts of variables can be shown to affect lexical access? One variable that has been studied extensively is **word frequency**. It appears that the frequency of occurrence of a word in the language affects the time it takes to gain access to that word in the mental lexicon. In general, the more frequently occurring words are accessed more quickly; and high-frequency words are more easily identified when they are presented in situations when they are hard to hear or see (Savin, 1963). This high-frequency advantage also shows up in cases where there is no stimulus degradation. Thus, we find that more frequent words are named faster (Forster and Chambers, 1973), classified faster (Frederiksen and Kroll, 1976), and matched faster (Chambers and Forster, 1975) than words which occur less frequently in the language.

A variety of studies have also demonstrated frequency effects in on-line sentence processing studies; one of these studies was done by Foss (1969). The subjects in Foss's experiment were asked to do two things. They heard a list of sixty unrelated sentences and had both to comprehend the sentences and to listen for a word in each sentence that began with the sound segment [b]. They were instructed to push a button as soon as they heard the word beginning with [b]. A timer was started as soon as the word beginning with [b] occurred in the sentence, and it was stopped by the subject's pushing the button. This kind of divided-attention task is called a *phoneme monitoring* task. Foss presented his subjects with sentences like these:

The travelling *b*assoon player found himself without funds in a strange town.
The itinerant *b*assoon player found himself without funds in a strange town.

The two sentences are identical except for the word that immediately precedes the 'target phoneme'. These two words are quite similar in meaning, but they differ quite a bit in their frequencies of occurrence in the language. *Travelling* is a word that occurs relatively frequently; *itinerant* has a relatively low frequency of occurrence. It is assumed, on the basis of a fair amount of evidence, that subjects' reaction times (RTs) in a phoneme monitoring task reflect the difficulty that subjects are having with sentence processing at the point where the target phoneme occurs. That is, if the process of comprehending the sentence is going along relatively smoothly at the point where the target occurs, the subject should be able to devote more processing capacity to the reaction-time task. If things are not going all that smoothly, we should expect that subjects would have less processing capacity to devote to reacting to the target phoneme, and we would expect to see relatively longer RTs to the target. Thus, where the sentence is easy to process, subjects' RTs should be faster.

Foss found that the average RT to respond to a phoneme target which followed a relatively low-frequency word was significantly longer than when the target followed a high-frequency word. Thus, subjects took longer to react to the [b] when it followed *itinerant* (in the example above) than they did to react to the phoneme when it followed *travelling*. Following the reasoning above, it would seem that the sentence processing mechanism is 'working harder' when it encounters low-frequency words than when it encounters high-frequency words. Thus, we have more evidence that word frequency affects the ease of lexical access.

We can imagine the mental lexicon as a list in which the more frequent words appear at the top of the list and the less frequent words appear toward the bottom. During lexical access, we can imagine that we search this list from the top to the bottom. Thus, we will find more frequent words more quickly because they appear relatively early on the list. But how does the lexicon come to be ordered in this way? There are a number of hypotheses about how we should interpret the frequency effects in lexical access.

One possibility is that more frequent words are, in some sense, more 'active' in the lexicon and that they can be more easily accessed (Morton, 1970). We might imagine that each time a word is pulled out of the mental lexicon it gets a little easier to pull out again. Thus, the more frequent words, because they are accessed more frequently, would become easier to get at. An analogy might help here. Suppose that each lexical entry were kept in a drawer and each time we encountered a word we opened up the drawer and examined the contents of the lexical entry. Suppose further that each time we opened up a drawer it opened a little more smoothly. The drawers that contained the more frequent words would eventually become easier and easier to operate, and we could get at their contents more easily than the drawers that were opened only once in a while. Thus, the frequency effects would result from differences in ease of lexical access, which would be determined by the frequency with which a word is encountered in the language.

Another possibility is that it is not frequency but *recency* that determines speed of lexical access. In this model we can imagine that the lexicon is like a big stack of lexical entries and that we search for a lexical entry starting at the top and moving toward the bottom. When we find the lexical entry we are looking for, we pull it out of the stack, get the information we need from it, and then put it back on the top of the stack. The lexical entries that we have had occasion to use most recently will be on the top of the stack. Since we will hear more frequent words more often, they will tend to occupy places toward the top of the stack. Thus, frequency of a word in the language will be a pretty good predictor of the relative place that that word will occupy in the list. (See Scarborough, Cortese and Scarborough, 1977; and Anderson, 1976, for more details and evidence for this model.)

Both of the models that we have discussed so far are *dynamic* models; that is, the position of the lexical entry in the list or the ease of access to the contents of the lexical entry will change over time. We can imagine *static* models, however, in which the place a lexical entry occupies does not change. One possibility for such a model is to assume that the position of a lexical entry on the list is determined by when it was learned (Carroll and White, 1973). Thus, words that you learned early in your linguistic career would appear at the top of the list, and new words would be put in at the bottom of the list. Frequency of a word in the language would be a good predictor of the relative place of that word in the list because we can assume that words that occur frequently in the language will be heard and learned sooner than words that occur infrequently. All of the models we have discussed seem to have their appealing aspects, and all of them have at least some empirical support. But, when all is said and done, it appears that we cannot point to one of them and say, 'That's the way to account for the frequency effects.'

Obviously, the mental lexicon must also be organized so

that the phonological properties of words can be used to guide the processes of lexical access; and there is evidence that words that sound the same are in some way grouped together in the mental lexicon (see Forster, 1976). This system might be looked upon as similar in certain respects to the system used in a standard dictionary: items that begin with the letter *a* are stored in one location, those beginning with *d* in another, etc. One problem with a completely phonologically organized system, though, is that is cannot account for the frequency effects that we have just discussed. A way out of this might be to assume that phonologically similar words are grouped together in sub-lists in the mental lexicon and that the positions of the words in these sub-lists are determined by their frequencies.

But there are still more problems. We pointed out earlier that the information in the mental lexicon must be accessed under a variety of different conditions: listening, speaking, reading and (possibly) writing. When we are reading, wouldn't it make sense to have words that are *spelled* in similar ways grouped together, just as we have argued that it makes sense for words that *sound* similar to be grouped together? And, since we seldom care about how words look or sound when we are constructing sentences (except in composing poetry), wouldn't it make sense to organize lexical entries according to semantic and syntactic similarity for the purposes of sentence production?

It would be very difficult – if not impossible – to organize the same set of lexical entries in a number of different ways without listing each entry in a number of different ways in a number of different locations in each of the different organizational schemes. This would be a somewhat inefficient use of space; so we might assume, following Forster (1976, 1979), that there is only one big lexicon where all

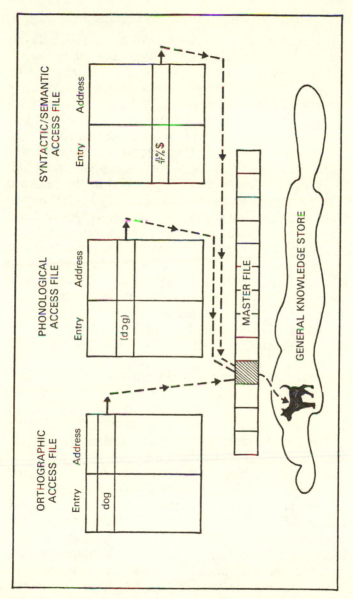

Fig. 8: An outline of the hypothesized organization of the mental lexicon (after Forster, 1976)

information about words is listed. We can refer to this as the *master file*. We can then assume that there are a number of *peripheral access files*, one organized by the phonological properties of words, one organized according to the orthographic properties of words, one organized according to syntactic/semantic properties of words, etc. The entry for each word in the master file will contain all the information we need to know about it; and the entry for each word in any of the peripheral access files will simply contain a description of the word in the relevant terms (i.e., phonological, orthographic, syntactic/semantic, etc.). Each entry in the peripheral access files will also have paired with it some sort of pointer or 'address' to the main entry for the word in the master file. Thus, we can assume that the information about a word that is contained in the master file is retrieved by a somewhat indirect route: we locate the appropriate entry for the word in the appropriate peripheral access file, find out the location of the entry in the master file, and then recover the information about the word that is contained in the master file.

This model of the mental lexicon is not so much like a dictionary as it is like a library. The problem that we have in a library is how to arrange things so that books can be reached efficiently in a variety of different ways. In a library we often want to find a book by a particular author, a book with a particular title, or a book on a particular subject; that is, we need to get at the books in the library via a number of different routes. One solution to this problem is to buy three copies of each book and to put each copy in a different section of the library; each section would then be organized according to a different principle. This is an inefficient use of space and money, so the solution that most libraries adopt is to buy just one copy of each book and to shelve all the books in one central location, organized according to some system like the Dewey Decimal System. The various books in the stacks can be accessed through a number of different catalogues (one organized by author, one by title, and one by subject); information contained in the catalogues includes an indication of the location of the book in the main collection. Thus, the books in the library are analogous to the entries in the master file of the mental lexicon, and the various catalogues are analogous to the peripheral access files.

As we noted above, the entries in each of the peripheral access files will be organized into groups according to their similarity across the relevant dimension. The places that the entries will occupy within these groups will be determined by their frequencies. This frequency may vary from file to file; e.g., the frequency of the written form of a word may be different from the frequency of its spoken form, and the appropriate frequency in the syntactic/semantic access file might be the frequency of occurrence of the word in the speech of the person whose lexicon it is.

It was thought for a while that the orthographic access file could be discarded. It was suggested that in reading, orthographic representations were converted by rule into phonological representations and that the access to information in the lexicon took place via the sound of the word. Now, however, it is generally agreed that the available evidence indicates that there is an independent orthographic access file (see Bradshaw, 1975; Marshall, 1976).

There is also some evidence that there must be some sort of system of cross-referencing the entries in the master file. Meyer and Schvaneveldt (1971), for example, have shown that lexical access is facilitated for a word if it is preceded by a related word. Thus, in a lexical access experiment the word *doctor* is reacted to more quickly if it is preceded by the word *nurse*. We might postulate a system for cross-referencing words that are related in meaning in the master file to account for this (Forster, 1976). Another possibility would be to assume that the master file does not contain very much information about the meanings of words, just a sort of bare-bones specification of meaning. The entries in the master file would then be assumed to be linked in some way to another big file of information about the world, how it is structured and how it works. Thus, in looking up the word *nurse* in the master file we would be referred to a part of our memory where all sorts of general knowledge about nurses is represented. This knowledge would include such things as the fact that nurses often work in hospitals, that doctors also work in hospitals, etc. Thus, the links between the two words could be made via a sort of general purpose file of information about the world. We might also assume that some of the 'semantic' operations, such as making inferences, are carried out on the basis of this general information store.

Up to now we have been discussing mainly those aspects of the lexicon that are related to comprehension; but what about production? We have one access file already in our model that is used in production – the syntactic/semantic access file. As we noted in Chapter 7, speech errors in which semantically and/or syntactically related words are substituted for one another in speech suggest that there is some sort of representation used by speakers that is based on such principles. We also mentioned the existence of **malapropisms** in that chapter. Fay and Cutler (1977) have shown that speech errors like the substitution of *monogamy* for *monotony* suggest that words are also organized according to phonological similarity for the purposes of speech production as well as perception. This indicates that we might need to add an additional access file to our model. It may be that there is a separate file in which the details of word pronunciation are represented and that this file is organized on the basis of phonological or articulatory similarity (Forster, 1976). Thus, words that begin with the same sequences of sounds, have the same number of syllables and have the same stress patterns would be grouped together in this file.

Summary

At this point we seem to have constructed a very complex model of the lexicon. At first glance, the system may seem quite baroque, but a moment's thought should convince you that organizing things in this way makes a lot of sense. Perhaps the strongest argument in favour of this model is that it seems to be counterproductive to organize the system in any other way. The system of various access files, each organized according to specific principles, is an efficient way to structure our model of the mental lexicon; and, after all, one of the most remarkable facts about the mental lexicon is the speed at which we can gain access to the information contained in it. The model also seems to be the one which most easily accounts for the sometimes bewildering body of evidence that suggests that the lexicon is organized in a variety of different ways. Having different sorts of information represented in different ways and in different places also seems to account for many facts that would be hard to explain in other models. For example, many of us can read words perfectly well but cannot spell those words correctly. If there were just one place where the spelling of words were represented for both perception and production, how could we explain this fact? A number of our colleagues have remarked that they often can only check the spelling of words in their students' papers by writing the words themselves and then comparing their written representations of the words with their students' spellings. This phenomenon, too, would be difficult to explain if there were only one listing of words with a single representation of orthographic information.

It appears, then, that the lexicon has a very complex structure, which allows us quickly and efficiently to 'look up' words via a number of 'special-purpose' routes.

9. Conclusion

It should be clear by now that understanding and producing speech is an amazingly complex business. It should also be clear that providing an explanation for how it is that people are able to accomplish this is a remarkably complicated business in its own right. The very fact that we have raised more questions than we have answered in this little book is an indication of just how hard it is and of how far we still have to go in providing such an explanation. We have seen that providing an explanation for people's abilities to speak and understand involves coming up with answers to two questions: what do the speakers of a language *know* about their language, and how do they put that knowledge to use when they listen and talk? We know a little about the answers to each of these questions now, so perhaps we should try to summarize.

A person who knows a language knows all sorts of things about that language. He or she knows what sounds are used by that language, how those sounds may be arranged to form words and morphemes in that language, what distinctions between sounds are meaningful, what the actual words are in the language, as opposed to the merely possible ones, how the words are arranged to form phrases, sentences and discourses, and on and on. The most important thing that we have pointed out about this knowledge is that it must be *productive*. Speakers of a language have the ability to produce all kinds of sentences that they have never produced or heard before, and hearers can understand all kinds of sentences that they have never heard or used before. Thus, we have seen that the knowledge that speakers and hearers have of their language must be represented as a system of *rules* that can describe an infinite set of sentences, the set of sentences that have been encountered and the set of sentences that may be encountered.

This knowledge of the language must also be *abstract*. We have seen that many of the things that language users know about their language are not explicitly marked. For example, consider the sentence

Kim likes little boys and girls.

This sentence is ambiguous. The ambiguity comes about because we can assign two different syntactic structures to the phrase *little boys and girls*:

(a) [little [boys and girls]]
(b) [[little boys] and [girls]]

The first structure corresponds to something like 'Kim likes little boys and little girls', and the second to something like 'Kim likes little boys and all girls'. The sentence itself does not carry information about its structure, so we must assume that hearers are able to *add* information to the strings of words that they hear. This additional information is based on the hearer's knowledge of the syntactic structure of his or her language; and, in this case, what the hearer knows about the language will 'tell' him or her that there are two possible syntactic structures that can be assigned to the string *little boys and girls*. This knowledge of the language is also put to use in filling in the 'gaps' that often appear in the sentences we hear and read, as in the case of missing subjects of infinitives (*John wants to go*) which we discussed above.

Because we seem to be committed to the view that hearers add information to the strings of sounds and words as they come in, we are also committed to the view that the

193

process of speech perception is an *active* process. That is, we cannot assume that the hearer just sits passively by, picking off the various cues in the speech stream. We must assume that hearers are actively using all the knowledge that they have at their disposal in the process of *reconstructing* the details of messages that they hear. We encountered this notion first when we discussed speech perception. There we discovered that it appears that hearers must use all sorts of knowledge in order to identify what sounds they are actually hearing, including, possibly, knowledge of how the vocal tract operates. The big problem in speech perception was, as we saw, that sounds that are perceived as being the same (for example, we hear a *b* at the beginning of both *big* and *bag*) are often acoustically distinct. That is, sounds that are acoustically different are perceptually identical. What we hear, then, is some sort of abstract representation. Thus, the process of comprehending involves the active *decoding* of some abstract representation of a message which the speaker has *encoded* in the speech stream.

We have tried to describe some of the properties that these abstract representations must have in this book, and we have also tried to describe the basic properties of the system that enables us to compute these abstract representations. Our readers will have noticed, however, that many of our answers have been either somewhat vague or extremely tentative. The past twenty-five years or so have seen many theories come and go, and it's quite reasonable to assume that in the next few years a lot of what we have said here will have to be changed. We have tried, however, to focus on those things which we feel we can be relatively confident of. Thus, we have focused on very general properties of language and language processing rather than on little details. What we have attempted is to provide an introduction to how psycholinguists go about doing their work and to what they believe they should do next on the basis of what they have learned so far.

Conclusion

Because there are many people working on the problems we have discussed here, some of the things we have said may already be out of date when you read this. Someone, somewhere, in his or her lab may be providing an answer to one of our questions. Someone else may have just shown that some experimental 'fact' is in actuality an artifact. Someone else may have just provided the critical test for some theory or some aspect of a theory and found it wanting. (For example, it appears that researchers at various places in the USA have succeeded in producing 'speech' through synthetic means that contains none of the traditional speech 'cues' and which could not possibly be produced by anything remotely resembling a human vocal tract but which is, nevertheless, perceived as speech [R.E. Remez, personal communication].) All of this makes the field very exciting, especially to one who is actively engaged in research. It does, however, make writing a book on the subject a little awkward. We hope that we have been able to spark the reader's interest in the subject and that we have been able to provide the reader with enough information and background to pursue that interest in the future.

References

Anderson, J. 1976. *Language, Memory, and Thought.* Hillsdale, New Jersey: Erlbaum.

Bastian, J., Eimas, P., and Liberman, A. 1961. Identification and discrimination of a phonemic contrast induced by silent interval. *Journal of the Acoustical Society of America*, 33.

Boomer, D., and Laver, J. 1968. Slips of the tongue. *British Journal of Disorders of Communication*, 3.

Bradshaw, J. 1975. Three interrelated problems in reading: a review. *Memory and Cognition*, 3.

Bransford, J., Barclay, J., and Franks, J. 1972. Sentence memory: constructive vs. interpretive approach. *Cognitive Psychology*, 3.

Bresnan, J. 1983. The passive in lexical theory. In J. Bresnan, ed., *The Mental Representation of Grammatical Relations*. Cambridge, Mass.: MIT Press.

Caplan, D. 1972. Clause boundaries and recognition latencies for words in sentences. *Perception and Psychophysics*, 12.

Carroll, J., and White, M. 1973. Word frequency and age of acquisition as determiners of picture-naming latency. *Quarterly Journal of Experimental Psychology*, 25.

Chambers, S., and Forster, K. 1975. Evidence for lexical access in a simultaneous matching task. *Memory and Cognition*, 3.

Chomsky, N. 1957. *Syntactic Structures*. The Hague: Mouton.

Chomsky, N. 1965. *Aspects of the Theory of Syntax*. Cambridge: MIT Press.

References

Clark, H., and Clark, E. 1977. *Psychology and Language.* New York: Harcourt Brace Jovanovich.

Cooper, F., Delattre, P., Liberman, A., Borst, J., and Gerstman, L. 1952. Some experiments on the perception of synthetic speech sounds. *Journal of the Acoustical Society of America*, 24.

Cutting, J., and Rosner, B. 1974. Categories and boundaries in speech and music. *Perception and Psychophysics*, 16.

Darwin, C. 1971. Ear differences in the recall of fricatives and vowels. *Quarterly Journal of Experimental Psychology*, 23.

Delattre, P. C., Liberman, A. M., and Cooper, F. S. 1955. Acoustic loci and transitional cues for consonants. *Journal of the Acoustical Society of America*, vol. 27.

Denes, P. B., and Pinson, E.M. 1973. *The Speech Chain: the Physics and Biology of Spoken Language.* Garden City, New York: Anchor.

Eimas, P., Siqueland, E., Jusczyk, P., and Vigorito, J. 1971. Speech perception in infants. *Science*, 171.

Fant, G. 1953. Discussion on the paper of G. E. Peterson: 'The information bearing elements of speech'. In W. Jackson, ed., *Information theory.* London.

Fay, D., and Cutler, A. 1977. Malapropisms and the structure of the mental lexicon. *Linguistic Inquiry*, 8.

Fodor, J. A. 1983. *On Modularity.* Cambridge, Mass.: MIT Press.

Fodor, J. A., Bever, T., and Garrett, M. 1974. *The Psychology of Language: an Introduction to Psycholinguistics and Generative Grammar.* New York: McGraw-Hill.

Fodor, J. A., Fodor, J. D., Garrett, M. F., and Lackner, J. R. 1974. Effects of surface and underlying clausal structure on click location. *Quarterly Progress Report 113.* Research Laboratory of Electronics, MIT.

Fodor, J. D. 1978. Parsing strategies and constraints on transformations. *Linguistic Inquiry*, 9.

198

References

Fodor, J. D. 1979. Superstrategy. In W. Cooper and E. Walker, eds., *Sentence Processing*. Hillsdale, New Jersey: Erlbaum.

Ford, M., Bresnan, J., and Kaplan, R. 1983. A competence based theory of linguistic closure. In J. Bresnan, ed., *op. cit.*

Forster, K. 1976. Accessing the mental lexicon. In R. Wales and E. Walker, eds., *New Approaches to Language Mechanisms*. Amsterdam: North-Holland.

Forster, K. 1979. Levels of processing and the structure of the language processor. In W. Cooper and E. Walker, eds., *Sentence Processing*. Hillsdale, New Jersey: Erlbaum.

Forster, K., and Chambers, S. 1973. Lexical access and naming time. *Journal of Verbal Learning and Verbal Behavior*, 12.

Foss, D. 1969. Decision processes during sentence comprehension: effects of lexical item difficulty and position upon decision times. *Journal of Verbal Learning and Verbal Behavior*, 8.

Foulke, E. 1971. The perception of time compressed speech. In D. Horton and J. Jenkins, eds., *Perception of Language*. Columbus, Ohio: Chas. Merrill.

Frazier, L. 1978. On comprehending sentences: syntactic parsing strategies. PhD dissertation, University of Connecticut. Indiana University Linguistics Club mimeo.

Frazier, L., Clifton, C., and Randall, J. 1983. Filling gaps: decision principles and structure in sentence comprehension. In *Cognition*.

Frederiksen, J., and Kroll, J. 1976. Spelling and sound: approaches to the internal lexicon. *Journal of Experimental Psychology: Human Perception and Performance*, 2.

Freud, S. 1974. *Introductory Lectures on Psychoanalysis*. J. Strachey, trans. Harmondsworth: Penguin Books.

Freud, S. 1975. *The Psychopathology of Everyday Life*. A. Tyson, trans. Harmondsworth: Penguin Books.

References

Fromkin, V. 1971. The non-anomalous nature of anomalous utterances. *Language*, 47.

Fromkin, V. (ed.) 1973. *Speech Errors as Linguistic Evidence*. The Hague: Mouton.

Fromkin, V. (ed.) 1980. *Errors in Linguistic Performance: Slips of the Tongue, Ear, Pen, and Hand*. New York: Academic Press.

Garrett, M. 1975. The analysis of sentence production. In G. Bower, ed., *The Psychology of Learning and Motivation* (vol. 9). New York: Academic Press.

Garrett, M. 1976. Syntactic processes in sentence production. In R. Wales and E. Walker, eds., *New Approaches to Language Mechanisms*. Amsterdam: North-Holland.

Gerstman, L. 1967. Classification of self-normalized vowels. *Proceedings of the IEEE Conference on Speech Communication and Processing*.

Goldman-Eisler, F. 1958. Speech production and the predictability of words in context. *Quarterly Journal of Experimental Psychology*, 10.

Harris, C. M. 1953. A study of the building blocks in speech. *Journal of the Acoustical Society of America*, 25.

Ladefoged, P. 1967. *Three Areas of Experimental Phonetics*. London: Oxford University Press.

Ladefoged, R., and Broadbent, D. 1957. Information conveyed by vowels. *Journal of the Acoustical Society of America*, 29.

Lashley, K. 1951. The problem of serial order in behavior. In L. Jeffress, ed., *Cerebral Mechanisms in Behavior*. New York: Wiley.

Lenneberg, E. H. 1967. *Biological Foundations of Language*. New York: Wiley.

Liberman, A. M. 1970. The grammars of speech and language. *Cognitive Psychology*, 1.

Liberman, A., Harris, K., Eimas, P., Lisker, L., and Bastian, J. 1961. An effect of learning on speech

200

perception: the discrimination of durations of silence with and without phonemic significance. *Language and Speech*, 4.

Liberman, A., Cooper, F., Shankweiler, D., and Studdert-Kennedy, M. 1967. Perception of the speech code. *Psychological Review*, 74.

Liberman, A., and Studdert-Kennedy, M. 1979. Phonetic perception. In R. Held, H. Leibowitz, and H.-L. Teuber, eds., *Handbook of Sensory Physiology*, vol. 8: *Perception*. Heidelberg: Springer-Verlag.

Liberman, M., and Prince, A. 1977. On stress and linguistic rhythm. *Linguistic Inquiry*, 8.

Lieberman, P. 1970. Towards a unified phonetic theory. *Linguistic Inquiry*, 1.

Lieberman, P. 1973. On the evolution of human language: a unified view. *Cognition*, 2.

Lieberman, P. 1975. *On the Origins of Language: an Introduction to the Evolution of Human Speech*. New York: Macmillan.

Lieberman, P., Crelin, E., and Klatt, D. 1972. Phonemic ability and related anatomy of the newborn and adult human, Neanderthaler man, and the chimpanzee. *American Anthropologist*, 74.

Lisker, L., and Abramson, A. 1964. A cross-language study of voicing in initial stops: acoustical measurements. *Word*, 20.

Lyons, J. 1981. *Language, Meaning and Context*. London: Fontana Paperbacks.

Maclay, H., and Osgood, C. 1959. Hesitation phenomena in spontaneous English speech. *Word*, 15.

Marshall, J. 1976. Neuropsychological aspects of orthographic representation. In R. Wales and E. Walker, eds., *New Approaches to Language Mechanisms*. Amsterdam: North-Holland.

Martin, J. G. 1967. Hesitations in the speaker's production and listener's reproduction of utterances. *Journal of Verbal Learning and Verbal Behavior*, 6.

References

Mattingly, I. 1976. Phonetic prerequisites for first-language acquisition. In W. von Raffler-Engel and Y. Lebrun, eds., *Baby Talk and Infant Speech*. Amsterdam: Swets and Zeitlinger.

Meyer, D., and Schvaneveldt, R. 1971. Facilitation in recognizing pairs of words: evidence of a dependence between retrieval operations. *Journal of Experimental Psychology*, 90.

Miller, G., and Chomsky, N. 1963. Finitary models of language users. In R. D. Luce, R. Bush and E. Galanter, eds., *Handbook of Mathematical Psychology* (vol. II). New York: Wiley.

Miller, G., Heise, G., and Lichten, W. 1951. The intelligibility of speech as a function of the context of the test materials. *Journal of Experimental Psychology*, 41.

Morton, J. 1970. A functional model of human memory. In D. Norman, ed., *Models of Human Memory*. New York: Academic Press.

Osgood, C. E. 1971. Where do sentences come from? In D. Steinberg and L. Jakobovits, eds., *Semantics*. Cambridge: Cambridge University Press.

Peterson, G., and Barney, H. 1952. Control methods used in a study of the vowels. *Journal of the Acoustical Society of America*, 24.

Peterson, G., Wang, W., and Sivertsen, S. 1958. Segmentation techniques in speech synthesis. *Journal of the Acoustical Society of America*, 30.

Radford, A. 1981. *Transformational Grammar: a Student's Guide to Chomsky's Extended Standard Theory*. Cambridge: Cambridge University Press.

Rand, T. 1971. Vocal tract size normalization in the perception of stop consonants. *Haskins Laboratory Status Reports on Speech Research*, SR-25/26.

Repp, B., Liberman, A., Eccardt, T., and Pesetsky, D. 1978. Perceptual integration of acoustic cues for stop,

References

fricative, and affricate manner. *Journal of Experimental Psychology: Human Perception and Performance*, 4.

Rohrman, N., and Gough, P. 1967. Forewarning, meaning, and semantic decision latency. *Psychonomic Science*, 9.

Sabol, M., and DeRosa, D. 1976. Semantic encoding of isolated words. *Journal of Experimental Psychology: Human Learning and Memory*, 2.

Savin, H. 1963. Word-frequency effect and errors in the perception of speech. *Journal of the Acoustical Society of America*, 35.

Scarborough, D., Cortese, C., and Scarborough, H. 1977. Frequency and repetition effects in lexical memory. *Journal of Experimental Psychology: Human Perception and Performance*, 3.

Shattuck-Hufnagel, S. 1980. Speech errors as evidence for a serial-ordering mechanism in sentence production. In W. Cooper and E. Walker, eds., *Sentence Processing: Psycholinguistic Studies Presented to Merrill Garrett*. Hillsdale, New Jersey: Erlbaum.

Skinner, B. F. 1938. *The Behavior of Organisms*. New York: Appleton-Century-Crofts.

Solan, L. 1980. Local processing and the grammar. Cornell University, mimeo.

Stark, R. 1979. Prespeech segmental feature development. In P. Fletcher and M. Garman, eds., *Language Acquisition*. Cambridge: Cambridge University Press.

Stevens, K., and House, A. 1955. Development of a quantitative description of vowel articulation. *Journal of the Acoustical Society of America*, 27.

Tannenbaum, P., Williams, F., and Hillier, C. 1965. Word predictability in the environments of hesitation. *Journal of Verbal Learning and Verbal Behavior*, 4.

von Békésy, G. 1960. *Experiments in Hearing*. New York: McGraw-Hill.

Wanner, E., and Maratsos, M. 1978. An ATN approach

to comprehension. In M. Halle, J. Bresnan, and G. Miller, eds., *Linguistic Theory and Psychological Reality*. Cambridge, Mass.: MIT Press.

Williams, E. 1979. Across the board rule application. *Linguistic Inquiry*, 9.

Index

abstractions, 71, 76f, 84
acoustic invariance, 43f, 48f, 59
active reconstruction, 40, 50, 54, 59
agreement, 134
articulation, 25, 35
  deviations from ideal positions, 27-8, 42-3
auditory nerve, 28, 31
auditory ossicles, 29, 30

babbling, 51, 52
basic word order, 66-7, 70

categorical perception, 49-50
clicks, 24
cochlea, 31
compounds, 72
conjunction, 72, 125f
consonants, 25, 36f
context, 17, 53-4, 64-5, 70, 107, 129, 145f
control, 99
conference, 99
creativity, 74-5, 80-1, 161

deep structure, 67f, 70, 71
deletion, 100f

development, 50f
diphthongs, 26

ear, 28-31
  ear canal, 30
  eardrum, 30
  inner ear, 31
  middle ear, 30-1
  outer ear, 30
echo question, 96

formant transition, 36, 46
formants, 35, 45f
fricatives, 24, 37-8, 48, 49-50

garden-path sentences, 61f, 141f
glides, vocalic, 26
grammar, 18, 63, 68, 70, 71

hair cells, 31
hesitations (see also pauses), 163f
HOLD, 87f, 92, 101, 102f, 108, 126

images, 159-60
imperative sentences, 77
implosives, 25

Index

incomplete information, use of, 64, 70, 87f
inference, 149f
infinities, 71f
intelligibility, 52, 53
introspection, 63
intuitions, 84, 106

larynx, 22, 23
late closure, 129f, 143
learning, 50f
left-to-right asymmetry in comprehension, 64-5
lexical access, 82, 182f
    frequency effects in, 182f
lexical ambiguity, 127f
lexical contributions to structure, 66, 105f
lexicon, 14, 16, 127, 139f, 142
    organization of, 176f, 181f
lips, 22, 23, 25, 26
    rounding of, 25, 26

meaning, 15, 16, 65, 70, 81-2, 143-4, 144f, 178, 180
mechanistic explanation, 83, 116f
memory, 87, 91f, 102f, 137
mind, 61, 71, 73, 114-15, 123-4, 155
modularity, 121f
morphemes, 179
    derivational, 179
    inflectional, 179
mouth, 22, 23

nasal cavity, 22, 23, 27

noun phrase, 80, 97
NP-movement, 90f

optional elements (in rules), 80
oval window, 30

parsing, 19, 69, 75, 87f, 113-14, 143f
pauses
    filled, 163, 164
    silent, 163, 164
personal qualities of speech, 44f
pharynx, 22, 23
phonetic description, 15
planning, 54f
    and neuronal firing order, 55
push-down stack, 92, 101

rate of transmission, 40-1, 43
redundancy, 37, 52f, 133f
reflexive pronouns, 77f
relative clause, 79
resonant frequency, 32-4, 35
resonating chamber, 32-4
response chaining, 57-8
    associative chain, 57
    behaviour chain, 57
retrieval of words, 82
rightward movement, 94f
rule, notion of, 18-19

segmentation, 16
semantic rules, 15, 17
serial ordering, 56

206

sound perception, 28
sound reception, 28
sound waves, 15
spectrogram, 33, 34, 35
spectrograph, 34
speech errors (slips of the
  tongue), 56f, 165f
  accommodations, 174-5
  anticipations, 167
  blends, 168, 173
  exchanges, 165-7, 169f,
    172-4
  malapropisms, 168, 172,
    190
  perseverations, 167-8
  semantic, 169, 172
  shifts, 167, 174
spoonerisms, 163, 165
stop consonants, 24, 37, 49
surface structure, 67f, 70, 71
syllable, 37, 42-3
syntax, 15, 17

tongue, 22, 23
  tongue body, 26

tongue position, 26, 35-6
trace, 68, 83
transformations
  (transformational rules),
  67, 68, 70, 71, 82f, 84f
  question formation, 68, 83

universals, 73, 79

velum, 22, 23, 27
verbs, 66, 70, 80, 105, 128,
  139f
vocal cords, 22, 23
vocal tract, 22, 23, 54
  as an acoustic filter, 32f
  development of, 51-2
voicing, 24, 37, 49
  voice onset time, 49
vowels, 25, 34f, 44f
  determinate vowels, 47-8
  point vowels, 48
  vowel space, 36, 47

whispering, 24

Another Universe book of related interest

THE ARTICULATE MAMMAL

Jean Aitchison

Is [language] a 'natural' phenomenon such as walking or sexual activity, or is it a skill which we learn, such as knitting? Why can parrots and myna birds mimic human speech although they don't understand it? Are babies born with a "blueprint" for language in their brains? In *The Articulate Mammal*, Jean Aitchison explores these and other questions that confront anyone who wants to know why we talk the way we do.

In her entertaining and informative book, the author studies slips of the tongue, speech disorders, and the language of normal adults to examine the link between what we hear and how we produce responses.

"Introduce[s] the topic of contemporary linguistics in a simple, straightforward, and intelligent manner...an excellent text." *—Choice*

"Both linguistics students and the general public should enjoy this readable introduction to psycholinguistics. Research in animal communication and theories of first-language acquisition by children are clearly presented and illustrated where necessary. The bibliography is extensive and includes the major authorities in the field. Much attention is devoted to the thinking of Noam Chomsky, though Aitchison by no means accepts all of his ideas uncritically. The book makes it quite clear that there are different schools of thought and that on many fronts, psycholinguistic research is in its infancy." *—Library Journal*

291 pp.   ISBN 0-87663-422-6

UNIVERSE INTRODUCTIONS TO LINGUISTICS
Other titles in the series

LANGUAGE CHANGE: PROGRESS OR DECAY?

Jean Aitchison

Why do New Yorkers disagree over the pronunciation of the word 'coffee'? Why is 'chicken' no longer the plural of 'chick'? Purists have been complaining about it for centuries, but the fact remains: language changes. Drawing on the latest research, Jean Aitchison points out that the process of language change is natural and inevitable, a product of a wide range of sociological and psychological factors. Her survey covers such topics as the role of child language, the birth of new languages, and the death of old ones.

"For sociologists, obviously concerned with living languages, and for the general reader or the linguist who is interested in the insights provided . . ., this is an excellent book."—**The Incorporated Linguist**

264 pp.

Forthcoming

LANGUAGE, MEANING AND CONTEXT
by John Lyons
Outlines recent theories of linguistic semantics and assesses their strengths and weaknesses, stressing the interlocking system upon which language is based.

SYNTAX TODAY
by Keith Brown
A popular, simple survey of the main lines of development in grammatical theory.

LANGUAGE AND SOCIETY
by William Downes
The interaction between the various social factors involved in sociolinguistics, from geographical location and ethnic origin to social class and sex.

UNIVERSE BOOKS
381 Park Avenue South New York, N.Y. 10016